Sadler's Wells dance house

Sadler's Wells

dance house

Sarah Crompton

First published in 2013 by Oberon Books Ltd
521 Caledonian Road, London N7 9RH
Tel: +44 (0) 20 7607 3637 / Fax: +44 (0) 20 7607 3629
e-mail: info@oberonbooks.com
www.oberonbooks.com

A catalogue record for this book is available from the British Library.

PB ISBN: 978-1-84943-062-3
E ISBN: 978-1-84943-511-6

Photographs copyright © the Photographers
Photographer credits are catalogued on page 128

The publisher has made every effort to trace the copyright holders of all images reprinted in this book. Acknowledgement is made in all cases where the image source is available, but we would be grateful for information about any image sources where they could not be traced.

Front and back cover images by Tristram Kenton

Printed and bound by Replika Press PVT, India.

Visit www.oberonbooks.com to read more about all our books and to buy them. You will also find features, author interviews and news of any author events, and you can sign up for e-newsletters so that you're always first to hear about our new releases.

Front Cover: Sylvie Guillem & Akram Khan in *Sacred Monsters*
Back Cover: Sidi Larbi Cherkaoui's *Sutra*
Page 2-3: Russell Maliphant's *The Rodin Project*
Page 6: Akram Khan in *DESH*

For Mary Crompton

CONTENTS

1   A NEW BEGINNING   7

2   AKRAM KHAN, SIDI LARBI CHERKAOUI   21
    AND THE CREATION OF *ZERO DEGREES*

3   SYLVIE GUILLEM   33
    AND THE ARRIVAL OF STAR POWER

4   SADLER'S WELLS AND THE WORLD   43

5   MATTHEW BOURNE   55
    AND WELCOMING AN AUDIENCE

6   WAYNE MCGREGOR   67
    AND THE SCIENCE OF DANCE

7   BREAKIN' CONVENTION   79
    AND THE GROWTH OF HIP HOP

8   CHRISTOPHER WHEELDON   91
    AND THE BALLETIC TRADITION

9   *IN THE SPIRIT OF DIAGHILEV* AND   103
    HOW TO COMMISSION NEW WORK

10 HOFESH SHECHTER AND THE FUTURE   115

    REFERENCES   127

    PHOTOGRAPHER INDEX   128

"Somebody must always be doing something new, or life would get very dull."

Ninette de Valois

1

A NEW
BEGINNING

New beginnings sometimes happen quietly, so no one really notices what is going on. But sometimes they are announced. On Monday March 7 2005, the new director of Sadler's Wells, Alistair Spalding, decided the time had come to make a splash.

He had been formally appointed artistic director four months earlier: this was his first chance to describe his vision for the future of a theatre that had been in existence, in one form or another, since 1683. What he

said to the journalists assembled in the foyer was quite simple: "You've got the National Theatre for drama, English National Opera for opera, and I want Sadler's Wells to perform the same function for contemporary dance."

It sounds innocuous but that hope has proved to be profoundly significant. People had been talking about a national dance house at least since Ninette de Valois first brought her fledgling ballet company to Sadler's Wells

in 1931. But no one since those heady early days had tried to turn this north London theatre into a creative powerhouse – a place that would not only receive work, but commission and encourage it. Yet that was precisely Spalding's intention. "It is time for us to start investing in the future of the form," he said.

Sitting next to him were five new associate artists: Matthew Bourne, the BalletBoyz, Jonzi D, Wayne McGregor and Akram Khan, the choreographers who would shape that future. Sidi Larbi Cherkaoui was also there. Yoking together Jonzi D, a leading force in British hip hop culture with the cerebral experimentation of McGregor, the rising talent of Khan, the worldwide fame of Bourne and the popularising instincts of BalletBoyz Michael Nunn and William Trevitt, this list revealed a wide-ranging taste. As Nunn recalled: "He grabbed everyone he could think of who had talent and was successful at the time." Debra Craine was duly impressed.

Above: Alistair Spalding announces the first associate artists in 2005
(*From left to right:* Sidi Larbi Cherkaoui, Akram Khan, Jonzi D, Mark Baldwin, Alistair Spalding, Matthew Bourne, Wayne McGregor, Michael Nunn and William Trevitt)

"It was like signing the entire England team in a single afternoon," she wrote in *The Times*.[1]

Two commissions were announced: the BalletBoyz would produce a piece called *Naked*, and the theatre would fund a new duet made by Khan and his Belgian contemporary Sidi Larbi Cherkaoui in collaboration with the sculptor Antony Gormley and composer Nitin Sawhney. But even as Spalding confidently announced his ambitions *The Sleeping Beauty on Ice* was running in the main auditorium. "We teased Alistair about that," remembered William Trevitt. "If you are presenting work that you are not totally comfortable with you don't have the same integrity, the same respect from everyone. Once the theatre starts to become a producing house, there is a whole different feel."

In fact Spalding had managed to plant some of the seeds of the developments to come. The Royal Ballet ballerina Sylvie Guillem and the BalletBoyz were due to return with an evening of choreography by Russell Maliphant. Pina Bausch had just presented *Nelken*, and the first Breakin' Convention was about to be launched. In the four months between his appointment and his season announcement, ticket sales rose by 40 per cent on the same period in the previous year and audiences were at a healthy 78 per cent.

As far as the BalletBoyz were concerned having office space in a theatre committed to creation was exactly what they were interested in. "We wanted somewhere we could call home that was about producing new work and encouraging collaborations which was what we had always been interested in," said William Trevitt.

What Sadler's Wells was doing was going back to the future. Spalding had instinctively recognised that the theatre had always been at its best when it was true to its origins. "There needed to be an artistic impetus for this thing to survive and when I looked back at the history that was always true. Sadler's Wells needed to have a focus and it needed to have a brand. I knew in my bones that to make it a creative dance house was the right thing to do."

The focus of London's second oldest theatre took some time to arrive. It was the discovery of a mineral spring in 1683 rather than any artistic impulse that led to its foundation. Over the centuries, it has been rebuilt five times, found popularity as a music house where singers, dancers and acrobats performed and notoriety as a drinking den. It has hosted a very young Edmund Kean and the great clown Grimaldi, and suffered conversion into a skating rink and a cinema. It has been reputable and unruly, pilloried and praised.

Above: Lilian Baylis, photographed by Carl Vandyk
Right: Flyer for *Twelfth Night*, signed by Lilian Baylis, John Gielgud and the cast

When people cite the inspiring history of Sadler's Wells, they are really talking about the period that begins in 1926 when a striking young Irish woman called Ninette de Valois went to see Lilian Baylis, the redoubtable manager of the Old Vic, and the woman who was ultimately responsible for the founding of the National Theatre, the English National Opera and, indirectly, The Royal Ballet. According to Kathrine Sorley Walker, Baylis was not at that point thinking of such grand plans. "She wanted a good, sensible (and cheap) dancing teacher who could help her actors and drama students to move rather better on stage and use their hands properly, someone who could arrange dances in plays and operas."[2] She also, though, did have at the back of her mind the idea of acquiring and re-opening Sadler's Wells. De Valois clearly impressed her. After their interview, her secretary Evelyn Williams recalled her saying: "That is all right. Miss de Valois is going to run her school with the Vic and when we have Sadler's Wells she'll run a wholetime ballet company for us."[3] The fact that it all came to pass says much about the abilities of both women.

After extensive fundraising, a reconstructed Sadler's Wells opened on January 6 1931 with a performance of *Twelfth Night* starring John Gielgud and Ralph Richardson. Thereafter drama productions, opera and ballet shuttled between the Old Vic and their new north London home. However, by 1935, the interchange ended; Sadler's Wells was dedicated to opera and ballet for

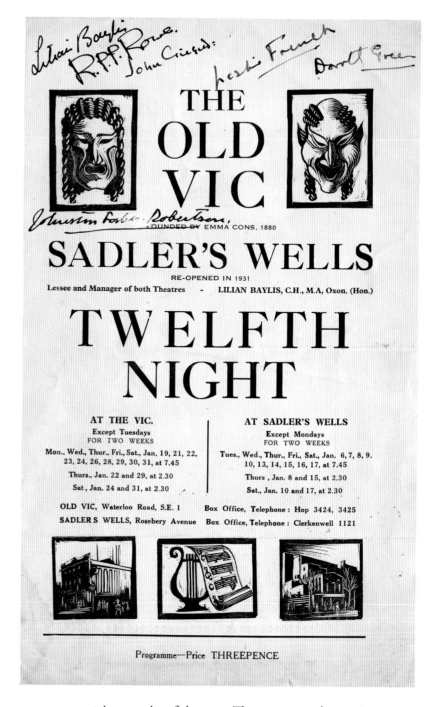

eight months of the year. The new season's opening night on September 27, was remarkable for " 'the splendid dancing of the young newcomer Miss Margot Fonteyn, who has a compelling personality and exceptional gifts', though only just 16."[4]

Although opera was always important at Sadler's Wells (it was on its stage that Britten's *Peter Grimes* premiered in 1945), for dance lovers it is this period that stamped it forever as a dance house. De Valois founded British ballet there, building not only a company of dancers, but a repertory too, commissioning new work from Frederick Ashton and her Australian leading man Robert Helpmann as well as creating her own still-performed works such as *The Rake's Progress*. She also founded a school, which remained there throughout all but three months of the war, when the theatre itself was commandeered as a refuge for the homeless. "When I entered the theatre each morning on my way up to the school quarters, I would encounter strange black shapes emerging from its depths," she wrote. "Large, fat, slow old women of Islington would seek the air they had breathed since birth."[5] The image of a company working through privation and hardship to inspire Britain with a love of ballet is enduring. De Valois recorded it herself, writing of the relentless touring through the war: "How our public grew! Everyone on war work went to the theatre and a vast, young public was ours, for children, up and down the country, were brought to the ballet as a means of bringing some light and relief into their broken up lives."[6]

In fact, although it is the pre-war and wartime period that attracts most attention, de Valois' relationship with Sadler's Wells persisted even after she had taken her fledgling company off to Covent Garden, where it became The Royal Ballet. The touring company, known as the Sadler's Wells Theatre Ballet, then the Sadler's Wells Royal Ballet, retained its links with the theatre. It was based there until 1955, and returned from 1970 to 1990, when it moved to Birmingham and became the Birmingham Royal Ballet. "Overshadowed to some extent from the beginning, Sadler's Wells Theatre Ballet was in fact to prove the hidden strength of de Valois' two organisations," judged Kathrine Sorley Walker. "From this smaller group came an army of dance talent, as well as two major choreographers, Kenneth MacMillan and John Cranko."[7]

The problem was that by the 1970s, the ballet company was not the sole occupant of Sadler's Wells. Rambert Dance Company and London Contemporary Dance were also briefly resident, which lent a sense of purpose, but the sheer variety of work booked to appear on its stage was confusing for everyone. For every great dance company such as Merce Cunningham, there was an indifferent show and through the 1980s, the diversity of attractions from Handel Opera to the Black Theatre of Prague, from Nederlands Dans Theater to Marcel Marceau began to baffle audiences. They started to stay away.

By the time Ian Albery took over as chief executive in 1994, it was clear that redefinition was needed. He came up with the visionary idea of applying to the newly-formed National Lottery for a grant to help him fulfil his dream of building a new theatre capable of housing world dance in the capital. The Arts Council agreed the plan and in 1998, after a two-year closure and a complete rebuilding, the current Sadler's Wells – the sixth theatre on the site – opened its doors, displaying an interior designed by RHWL and an exterior by Nicholas Hare. The £54 million project, achieved with the help of £42 million from the National Lottery, incorporated the skeleton of Frank Matcham's 1931 theatre (which itself contained bricks from the Victorian playhouse) behind its new transparent frontage. "The flesh was replaced but the bones beneath remain," explained architectural writer Hugh Pearman.[8] As patron of the Appeal, de Valois,

Left: The fifth Sadler's Wells building in 1935

Interior of the new Sadler's Wells main house

who had just celebrated her 100th birthday, wrote of her delight at the theatre's re-opening, since "I am sure it will come as no surprise to you to learn that Sadler's Wells holds a very special place in my heart." She added that in 1931 "we had not only to train a company but also to develop an audience. As our skill and repertory expanded over the years, so did our following."[9]

These proved to be premonitory words. The opening season was thrilling: it brought the great dance pioneer Pina Bausch back to London and William Forsythe's ground-breaking Ballett Frankfurt to the theatre for the first time, as well as establishing links with companies who would become popular regulars such as Rambert Dance Company. But thereafter, Sadler's Wells struggled to find its voice and its audience. When Albery left in October 2002, he was replaced by Jean-Luc Choplin, whose background was an odd mixture of Disney and European art house. Choplin's vision for Sadler's Wells was ambitious in scale but financially flawed – a show from avant-garde theatre director Robert Wilson flopped; the great mezzo soprano Jessye Norman cancelled. Spalding, who arrived when he was appointed as director of programmes in 2000, found himself confronted by grim financial realities.

By the time Spalding took over the artistic programme in 2004, the theatre was losing £50,000 a month and

playing to audiences of 65 per cent. London's paper, the *Evening Standard*, announced: "Stranded and unloved on a windy corner near the Angel, Islington, Sadler's Wells seemed…to have lost its point. After decades of slow decline, not averted by a new theatre…it had no artistic imperative, no clear identity and dwindling audiences."[10] Handed the top job (at first on a temporary basis) and charged with turning things around, Spalding concluded that Sadler's Wells had been at its best when it had had resident companies and new work being made within its walls. "For me it is incredibly important that any arts organisation had artists working in it. It changes the feel of the place."[11]

Alistair Spalding is an unlikely dance champion. He trained as a teacher and fell into arts administration

Above: Dame Ninette de Valois watching pupils at Sadler's Wells Ballet School in April 1931
(Photo by Sasha/Stringer/Hulton Archive/Getty Images)
Right: The sixth Sadler's Wells building

because he thought he might be better at it than he was at teaching. He started his career in Crawley and in 1994 took on the task of dance programming at the Southbank Centre. He has the emollient demeanour of a civil servant or an accountant, yet this disguises both a fierce passion for dance – which he watches up to four times a week – and a willingness to back hunches, instincts and beliefs with long-term investment. His arrival changed the fortunes of the theatre, not least because of his pragmatic ability to balance the books. One of his first acts, when he arrived in 2000, was to schedule the RSC's *The Lion, the Witch and the Wardrobe* to enable the theatre to make money over the Christmas period. Once in charge, he mixed the popular and the esoteric, and, remarkably, found audiences for both.

Finding an audience is important to Sadler's Wells, since the proportion of its Arts Council England grant as related to revenue (approximately 10 per cent) has not changed over the years. However, because audience numbers have increased, revenue itself has soared. In 2001, the grant stood at £900,000 out of total revenue of around £9 million. By 2012, it represented about the same percentage, but stood at £2.3 million, out of total revenue of £23 million. An impressive 70 per cent of that income came from the box office, a reflection of the fact that between 1999 and 2011 ticket sales had risen by 72 per cent, with more than half a million tickets sold in 2011. The rest of the income came from fundraising, rentals and catering.

The 1990s rebuilding prepared the ground for such success. The new theatre had a sprung stage that was 15 metres square instead of 10. The economic necessity to preserve a main house with 1,500 seats produced an unexpected bonus: the seats are close enough together to

give the audience a sense of community, a warmth noticed by the performers on stage. Sight lines are excellent; the décor of the house is both stylish and neutral so that nothing detracts from the action on stage. Furthermore, cultivated by the indefatigable John Ashford at The Place, and Val Bourne at Dance Umbrella, a new generation of choreographers were ready to emerge. What they needed was a stage – and an audience.

The viewers arrived on the back of a boom in interest in dance in Britain, a country always assumed to be keener on theatre than the more plastic arts. Yet by the mid 2000s, dance had imposed itself on the culture in a way that had not been seen since de Valois' wartime tours. According to the Arts Council, more than 13 per cent of the British population was attending some form of dance performance.[12] In 2008/9, the art form with the most significant increase in the number of performances, exhibition days and film screenings was dance, with a 39 per cent increase on the previous year.[13]

The makers of television programmes began to reflect the rising popularity of dance in their schedules. By 2009, the BBC's *Strictly Come Dancing* was regularly attracting 10.5 million viewers and the dance group Diversity had become the second dance act in succession to win *Britain's Got Talent*. Suddenly the word dance did not seem so frightening and exclusive anymore.

All of this helped to create an environment in which Sadler's Wells could thrive: between 2004 and 2012 its audience doubled. It has achieved such success partly thanks to commercial acumen. Its director of communications, Kingsley Jayasekera, arrived at the theatre just after Spalding, bringing with him a background in both dance (at Rambert) and in the commercial theatre (with the powerful Dewynters advertising agency).

He transformed the theatre's marketing, inventing the "Sadler's Wells is Dance" slogan, and helping its broad range of work to thrive by offering multibuy ticket offers, which encouraged audiences to try the new – and, crucially, to return over and over again to the theatre.

Such strategies enabled Sadler's Wells to put originality ahead of playing it safe. Even in its more assertively "populist" venue, the Peacock Theatre, which it rents from the London School of Economics, it has backed original material including the musical extravaganza *Shoes*. Its early investment in hip hop has been rewarded by its development as a commercial art form in shows such as *Some Like It Hip Hop*.

In its main house, it takes risks with new productions from its associate artists and guests. Many have been critical and commercial hits. Some have disappointed. Some have – as Zoë Anderson noted in the *Independent* – been "howlingly self-indulgent".[14] But the vast majority were significant, talked about, and made dance seem important again. Sadler's Wells has claimed a place at the top table of conversations about culture. Significantly, when *The Times* came to pick its dance face of the decade in 2010, it chose Spalding. "He has commissioned and facilitated more new contemporary dance than anyone else in Britain."[15] His CBE in 2012 acknowledged his significance.

Above: Sadler's Wells in 2008, celebrating 10 years since its rebuild

For Spalding this put the wrong face in the frame. "I wouldn't be sitting here if it wasn't for the artists. All I am doing is giving them the conditions to make the best of their work. In the end, the artist is king and if I don't look after their needs then there is no point in my being here."[16] Since his initial appointments in 2005, he has gathered 15 associate artists into the theatre, including Russell Maliphant, Sylvie Guillem and Hofesh Shechter. There are three resident companies: Wayne McGregor | Random Dance, New Adventures and ZooNation Dance Company. The work they have collectively produced has won awards and converts to contemporary dance. But they have also, as Spalding hoped, altered the spirit of the building.

When the American choreographer William Forsythe was working on *Rearray*, a new duet for Guillem and Nicolas Le Riche, he discovered that the Pet Shop Boys were working on *The Most Incredible Thing*, a collaboration with the choreographer Javier De Frutos in the studio next door. He was thrilled. "It is one of those places where you can meet anyone and everyone," he said. "It is a creative hub: people take it seriously and expect quality from it."

Where de Valois built a company of dancers and creators, Sadler's Wells has created a company of artists, dance-makers who are creating a new era of contemporary dance, and a new chapter in the history of the theatre itself. Michael Nunn summed up its effect: "It is incredible when you think about how important this place is for dance in the UK. It is the most important place." "It has become what it said it was going to be," said William Trevitt. "It created a sort of self-fulfilling prophecy. It is the dance house."

Above: Foyer of the new Sadler's Wells

2

AKRAM KHAN, SIDI LARBI CHERKAOUI AND THE CREATION OF *ZERO DEGREES*

Akram Khan was sitting in the sunshine outside Sadler's Wells with his friend Sidi Larbi Cherkaoui on the morning of July 7 2005. It was a beautiful day, and the two men were waiting to begin a dress rehearsal of their first choreographic collaboration, *zero degrees*. Then they noticed people walking down the centre of the street. The crowds were moving aimlessly, as if they had no place to go. The effect was frightening and disturbing – "like a zombie movie," said Khan – but they had no idea of the cause. It was only when Alistair Spalding arrived, his own journey to work interrupted by the events unfolding around him, that they understood that four explosions had ripped through three tube trains and a bus. Later still, they knew that the blasts, which left 52 people dead and more than 770 injured, were the work of suicide bombers.

In spite of the shock they, like everyone in London, felt they had to make practical decisions. Should they continue to rehearse and open the show the next night as planned? Spalding did not have much doubt about the pertinence of the work: "There could be nothing more appropriate than this piece." But was it right to go ahead and perform when the headlines were full of horror? Would anyone want to come to the theatre to see a new dance work in such terrifying times? The following evening the first preview provided the answer. With London's transport system still in chaos, bicycles covered the railings opposite the theatre, reaching higher and higher as more people arrived. The house was almost full.

Khan describes *zero degrees* as "the reference point where everything begins and everything ends."[1] It is a work about borders and belonging, about identity, about the self and otherness, about life and death. At one point in it, Khan speaks of finding a body on a train and on that night, as he said the words, the audience collectively seemed to draw breath, in a kind of pain and recognition. "It felt as if the story were taken out of us and belonged to them."

The emotional circumstances of its premiere apart, *zero degrees* was always going to be a pivotal piece for Spalding's commissioning policy at Sadler's Wells. When he announced his "new beginnings" policy, this was one of the works in which he invested most faith. He had watched Khan's choreography over a period of years and had offered him the chance to come to Sadler's Wells when he was ready. This was the moment. In an interview with Janet Street Porter, on Bloomberg TV, he pointed up its significance. Describing Khan as "a young South Asian dancer based in London but with a growing international reputation," he explained that the piece was a collaboration not only with Cherkaoui, but also with the sculptor Antony Gormley and the composer Nitin Sawhney. "This is a sign of where we want to go in future."[2]

In fact, the piece originally sprang from an encounter which did not involve either Spalding or Sadler's Wells. Khan and Cherkaoui met in 2000 when Khan was looking for dancers for his own company. Two things were immediately clear: firstly, that Cherkaoui was at a point in his own choreographic career where he did not need to work for someone else and secondly that they really liked each other.

Their backgrounds mark common ground. Akram Khan was born and brought up as a Muslim in London, to a family of Bangladeshi origin. Sidi Larbi Cherkaoui was born in Antwerp to a Flemish mother and a Moroccan father and attended an Islamic school for a

few hours each week. Both therefore, to some extent, feel part of and separate from the societies in which they grew up. Neither drinks. Both are workaholics. But their differences are equally significant. From the age of seven, Khan had trained in the Indian classical dance form kathak, to which he added the discipline of contemporary dance from the age of 22. These twin influences forged a style which is strongly rooted in the kathak tradition yet also recognisably modern. In addition, the experience of working with Peter Brook, who cast him, at the age of 14, as the Boy in his production of *The Mahabharata* made him believe that theatre should aim for simplicity, and should draw attention to the communicative powers of the body.

Above: Akram Khan and Sidi Larbi Cherkaoui in *zero degrees*

Cherkaoui, on the other hand, became hooked on the dance he saw in music videos and on television, but only began dancing at the relatively late age of 16. He became a dancer on television and at the same time took various dance classes including ballet, hip hop, tap, jazz and flamenco. After winning a talent contest organised by Alain Platel, founder of the dance collective les ballets C de la B, he signed up to contemporary classes at P.A.R.T.S., the school founded by the radical Belgian choreographer Anne Teresa De Keersmaeker. In 1997, he joined les ballets C de la B and was strongly influenced by their theatrical style.

The year 2000 was hugely significant for them both. Khan founded his own company, with the producer Farooq Chaudhry; Cherkaoui unveiled *Rien de Rien*, his ground-breaking full-length creation described as "a piece of such diverse range that it seemed to recalibrate the co-ordinates of 21st-century dance theatre".[3] Two

years later, Khan made his own breakthrough in the full-length *Kaash,* with a set designed by Anish Kapoor and music by Nitin Sawhney; the piece was an early indication of Khan's impulse to collaborate with the best artists in other fields. But it also revealed the range of his preoccupations: taking as his title the Hindu word for "if", he fashioned a meditation on the beginning and end of all things, with references to Hindu gods, black holes and Indian time cycles.

As their respective careers developed, the two men watched each other's progress, staying in touch, discussing ideas, and formulating a plan to work together. So when in 2003, they finally went into a studio for a month – first in Montreal and then in Vooruit-Gent – they knew that their collaboration would be grounded in a deep admiration of the other's vision. But they also recognised that this would be a meeting of opposites, a collision of Khan the purist and Cherkaoui the magpie,

Above: Akram Khan and Sidi Larbi Cherkaoui in *zero degrees*

between one man whose style was strongly rooted and another who had the chameleon-like ability to absorb the ideas of others and transform them into something uniquely his own. "We start from completely opposite poles," Khan said. "He starts from theatre and moves towards movement; I start from movement and work towards theatre. I'm hoping we meet halfway."[4]

For Khan, this period of intense creativity was like playtime, offering a chance to explore different possibilities with no end in view. They began by learning each other's choreographic technique, discovering as they did so that when Cherkaoui choreographed natural gestures into a language, the result resembled the hand movements used in kathak to tell stories. But the key moment came when Cherkaoui, quite simply, asked Khan to tell him something he had never told anybody before and Khan responded with the story of a journey he made to Bangladesh when he was a dance student in 1998. Travelling with his cousin, he initially refused to pay a bribe to a border guard as they crossed into India by train, but was intimidated into it. Then, a few stops later, he discovered a dead body, the first he had ever seen. He wanted to help the man's screaming wife, but his cousin stopped him. "He told me if I touched the body then the police would blame me for the man's death," Khan said. "Everyone was too scared to do anything. It was awful."[5]

This tale, woven into a narrative, became the bedrock of the piece. But for some time after that productive month of experiment, it looked as if *zero degrees* would not come to fruition because it did not have financial backing. That was when Spalding entered the picture. Hearing that Khan and Cherkaoui had an idea they wanted to develop, he offered them the means to stage it in the form of a co-production with Sadler's Wells.

At that point, the rest of the creative team came on board. Khan had worked with the composer Nitin Sawhney before, on *Fix* in 2001 and on *Kaash*, so he knew he wanted him to provide the score – a characteristically eclectic blend of many sounds, from Indian voices to classical instruments, from tabla rhythms to pop beats. He had also been talking to the sculptor Antony Gormley about making a piece together. Gormley, a dance fan, was keen to see what a world-famous visual artist could contribute to the dance stage. Once he heard what Khan and Cherkaoui had devised in the studio, his passion for the project increased: he believed that the story they had developed had a timeless universality which others would recognise.

In interviews at the time, Cherkaoui described this as a dream team. "[We are] people on a journey but in different places, who say similar things through different art forms."[6] But inevitably the ten weeks of intense creation that preceded the premiere was not entirely smooth. Initially, Khan was too prescriptive in his descriptions of what he wanted from Gormley. "I told him I needed a tree but then I realised that was not collaboration." Later, though, he resisted Gormley's inclination to complicate his grey-box setting. "He would come in through one door with an object and I would open the other door and take it out. I tried to protect the simplicity, so that was when the friction came."

Ultimately, they had such respect for each other that they found a way through their disagreements. Khan described it as "giving space to each other, and then letting the work decide." His description makes the

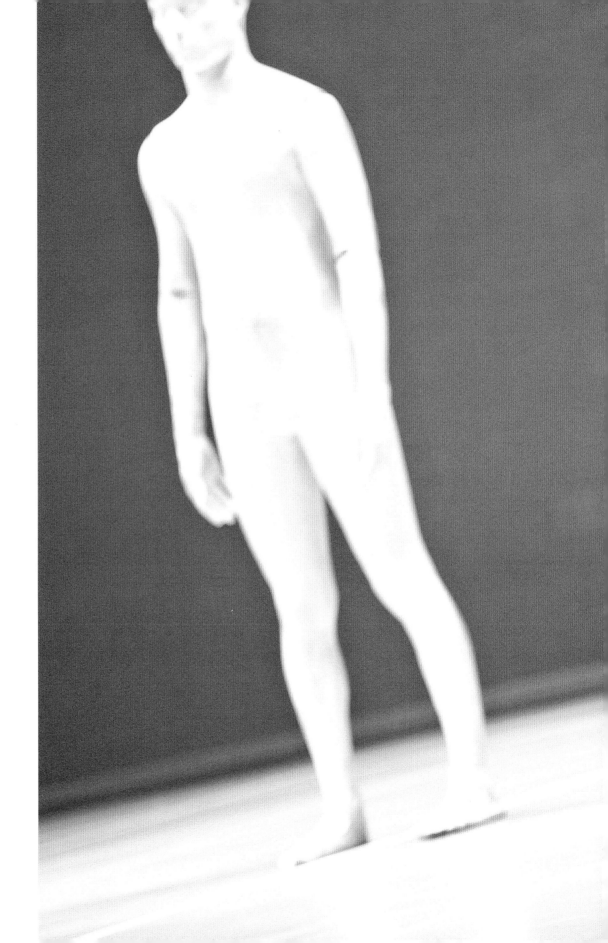

Right: Sidi Larbi Cherkaoui
in *zero degrees* with cast by
Antony Gormley

process sound almost mystical. "You have four opinions on one idea, but if you just keep going, the idea somehow stays, or the piece protects it. Then suddenly we all have to go OK."

It would be easy to underestimate the impact of Gormley's eventual contribution: two life-sized white casts of the two dancers, which could be strewn on the stage, or manipulated to stand watchfully by. Their inanimate, lifeless presence gave an eerie otherness to the work. Were they the dancers' alter egos, or reflections of past lives, gone and much regretted? Did they represent souls or bodies? Their very mysteriousness added resonance. In the same way, the white line along the centre of the stage and the musicians appearing faintly through gauze at the back, bolstered the metaphorical intention of the choreography unfolding in the space.

At the premiere on July 12 2005, it was clear that *zero degrees* was a strongly individual contemporary dance work. For one thing, Khan and Cherkaoui emerged purposefully from the wings, and sat cross-legged at the very front of the stage, their heads resting on their hands at exactly the same angle – and then immediately started speaking. Not only that, but they were telling a story – and telling it in perfect unison, their stylised gestures matching the pattern and shape of the words. When they started to move, it was the contrasts between them that were so striking: Cherkaoui was almost clumsy in his sneakers but flexible and weightless as a snake, with the ability to tie his body into knots; Khan spun on the spot and scampered around with a grounded grace, the rapid precision of his movements so sharp it was as if he were slicing the air with a knife.

In 70 minutes, neither man left the stage. They danced together, in movements of communion and of battle, and in solos where their only accompaniments were Sawhney's haunting music and the shadows that their bodies threw on the walls. They danced too with those casts, bringing them to life as partners in the dance. At the very end, Cherkaoui sat at the front of the stage, singing softly, cradling a broken dummy across his knee while Khan danced a lament of almost unbearable sadness. Suddenly his entire body begins to shake. He looks as if he is about to dissolve. Finally he falls to the ground, and Cherkaoui gently places his limp body over his shoulder and walks off, leaving the stage to the musicians, who ended the work on a mournful, dying fall.

In rehearsal, this ending had prompted the most debate. Khan was passionately committed to it; the others were less sure. Yet in the theatre the moment was devastating. Judith Mackrell in the *Guardian* remarked: "It is a conclusion that feels profound and perfunctory and it encapsulates the logic of the entire piece…Somehow these four artists have figured out that it's only by being provisional and exploratory that *zero degrees* gets as close as it does to the big themes – of love and loneliness, life and death."[7]

Mackrell also analysed the quality that made *zero degrees* special. "It began life as a private dialogue, just two dancers swapping ideas in the studio and what makes it so riveting in performance is that the intimacy which Khan and Cherkaoui discovered in rehearsal is etched so deep into the finished product."[8] This chimed strongly with Khan's own belief, that the piece sprang not from a rehearsal period of ten weeks, or even from the improvisational month before that, but "had been 20 years in the making. I have been training from childhood; Sidi Larbi has been training from childhood. All of that culminated in *zero degrees*."

As if in recognition, *zero degrees* was an instant hit with audiences. In 2005, it left Sadler's Wells on a pre-planned tour of five European capitals, returning to even greater acclaim in 2006 and 2007, before touring to 19 countries, including Argentina, Mexico,

Australia and the USA. It was the first Sadler's Wells commission not only to prove its worth artistically, but also to make money for the theatre – which Spalding then invested in commissioning more new work.

Extraordinary though it is in itself, *zero degrees* also marked the start of something bigger. It proved that Sadler's Wells could produce a work that had its own distinctive

Above: Akram Khan and Yoshie Sunahata in *Gnosis*

stamp. Spalding recognised this when he told Khan after the first performance: "this is the benchmark for the way we should work."

It was also the first flowering of a new kind of contemporary dance, one that reached beyond any particular style into the pioneering territory of experiment. "What I saw in Akram is that he embraced everything that he had learned – and just went beyond that," Cherkaoui said. "It is not about fighting tradition. Contemporary art is just a continuation of traditional art."[9] The words he applied to Khan could just as easily apply to Cherkaoui himself – and both men have helped to give Sadler's Wells a new reputation as a place that is prepared to absorb all the traditions of the past and take them in radical new directions. Separately, and in collaboration with others, they have provided the theatre with some of its most distinctive works.

The following year, Khan created *Sacred Monsters*, in which he and the ballerina Sylvie Guillem analysed and reassessed the classical traditions from which they sprang. This was followed by works he made for his company: *bahok* (2008) which continued to explore the themes of borders and boundaries expounded in *zero degrees* and the visceral *Vertical Road* (2010), a meditation on the difficulties of following a spiritual path amidst the distractions of modern life. *Gnosis* in 2010 was a return to more traditional territory, but then in 2011 Sadler's Wells co-commissioned *DESH*, an extraordinary autobiographical solo that seemed to fill the stage with people, even though Khan was dancing there alone. It was one of the best works he had ever made, full of humour, emotion, magic and poignant insight. For Khan, it was the first work since *zero degrees* that absolutely revealed his distinctive personal vision.

Left: Akram Khan in *DESH*

In 2008, Cherkaoui also became an associate artist and his contribution has been equally consistent. In *Sutra* (2008) and *Babel* (2010) he continued to work with Gormley, in the first accompanied by the monks of the Shaolin temple and a set of evocative wooden boxes, in the second, by an installation of steel cages that became towers and rooms. In 2009, with María Pagés he made the flamenco-flecked *Dunas*, once again performing alongside an artist whose fierce style contrasted strongly with his supple skills. In 2011 he returned to work with Sawhney on *TeZukA*, inspired by the visionary Japanese manga artist and animator Osamu Tezuka. His links with the theatre have also enabled him to take on smaller projects, such as charmingly fluid light-hearted cameos for Richard Thomas's crowd-pleasing *Shoes*, and *Faun* in an evening of works inspired by Diaghilev in 2009.

It is the imaginative span of Khan and Cherkaoui's engagement with Sadler's Wells that is so noticeable. In bringing them to the theatre as associate artists, the theatre has made a patient, long-term investment in their careers. With one eye on the need to make money and the other on the work, Spalding has been prepared to give them creative freedom, to let them push the limits of what is possible. In return, they have filled its stage with their dreams, and their belief in the range and variety of stories that dance can tell. They are ambitious dance-makers in the very best sense. And it all started with *zero degrees*.

Above: Monks from the Shaolin Temple in Sidi Larbi Cherkaoui's *Sutra*

3

SYLVIE GUILLEM AND THE ARRIVAL OF STAR POWER

Above: Sylvie Guillem in *Sacred Monsters*

The continuing journey of Sylvie Guillem is one of the most fascinating narratives within the story of Sadler's Wells. She is without doubt the most glamorous of all the associate artists at Sadler's Wells, with the pulling power of a star.

Yet at this distance, it is easy to underestimate just how far Guillem travelled by making the journey from the red plush of the Royal Opera House to a north London street. Because she has turned herself from an exceptional classical dancer into an equally illustrious contemporary one, it seems an obvious progression. But it certainly was not at the time. Driven always by a questing intelligence and a deep curiosity about the expressive capacity of dance, throughout her career first with Paris Opera Ballet and then The Royal Ballet in London, she longed to perform new work which would extend the creative potential of what it was possible to say through dance.

Knowing this, Michael Nunn and William Trevitt, better known as the BalletBoyz, who had left The Royal Ballet because they too felt creatively stifled by the company's reluctance to try new things, invited her to watch them dance with their new company George Piper Dances at The Place. The Boyz were early pioneers of a revolution to make dance both more accessible and more exciting to a wider audience: their performances were introduced by jokey backstage films. But it wasn't just their larky manner that won them admirers. They were both superb dancers, with an instinct for choosing new work of real merit.

On the night Guillem came to The Place, they were performing a programme including a duet called *Torsion*, made for them by a choreographer called Russell Maliphant, which exhibited his signature combination of strength and softness, serenity and power. The effect on

Guillem was "instinctive and physical". "I wished that I was onstage with them. I wanted to be part of it. It was kind of a call."[1] As a result of that encounter she produced a piece for herself and the Boyz which – in a unique arrangement – would be produced by George Piper Dances but performed on the stage of the Royal Opera House. *Broken Fall*, which premiered in December 2003, showed Guillem in an entirely new light, using her gymnastic daring in an intricate series of tumbling plunges, trusting the two men to catch and hold her. At the close, Guillem was alone on stage, in a contemplative sinuous doodle of a solo. It was sensational.

Guillem did not find it easy to learn Maliphant's style. "Every kind of style, even classical, you always hurt yourself for the first two weeks. It is part of the process." The rehearsals had been bruising; Trevitt remembered there was one particular step that she had struggled with. "She had to go from kneeling down to standing up by throwing one leg behind her." She practised it over and over again, until she "cracked it".[2] Guillem did however recognise that in some profound way, Maliphant's choreography suited her, allowing her to discover new ways of moving. Yet for all its success, *Broken Fall* only ran for five nights at Covent Garden, so Nunn and Trevitt were keen to give it another life. They were about to become associates at Sadler's Wells, involved in planning a new work for the forthcoming season, and so they mentioned their idea to Spalding. He in turn mentioned it to a colleague in Holland who was looking for something to open his festival in Amsterdam. "I suddenly thought, 'What am I doing? This should be a piece for Sadler's Wells.'"[3]

So it was that in October 2004, Sylvie Guillem arrived at Sadler's Wells in a programme of work dedicated to the choreography of Russell Maliphant. It featured *Torsion*, *Broken Fall*, and Guillem in a solo called *Two*, originally created for Maliphant's wife Dana Fouras. "I almost believed I saw sparks," wrote Jenny Gilbert in the *Independent on Sunday*.[4] "If this is a preview of the new Sylvie Guillem, I can't wait to see what's next." In the *Guardian*, Judith Mackrell declared: "Guillem may be approaching 40, but it is possible that the most extraordinary phase of her career has just begun."[5]

Guillem was indeed at a turning point. In interviews she hinted that her future with The Royal Ballet, the company that had been her base since she arrived from Paris Opera Ballet in 1988, was uncertain. Her desire to face new challenges had been frustrated by the company; if she wanted to move forward, it had to be outside The Royal Ballet. In an interview with Debra Craine in *The Times* she explained exactly why Maliphant's choreography held such a strong appeal for her. "Each moment was surprising me and I like not knowing what is coming next. His piece was also so quiet, so soft and serene. It was peaceful but at the same time it was really strong…the combination was quite striking."[6] Guillem's interest in creating work has always been driven by her desire for discovery. "I am interested in the sensation I can have doing it. I want to have the physical and mental experience of a new way of moving." This was the quality she valued in William Forsythe; it was also what she saw in Maliphant. "They are creative people and I want to go into their world, into their mind and also the way they see me. That is what is important."[7]

Beyond this she had no particular plan. "It was part of an evolution. Not a decision." Upon one thing, however, she was very insistent: for their next work together she actually wanted to dance with Maliphant. "When you try things with him, the body understands right away. He is a fantastic mover. I knew that when I danced with him it was luminous. I wanted to have that on stage."

Canadian-born Maliphant's links with Sadler's Wells went back to his earliest days as a dancer with the Sadler's Wells Royal Ballet from 1982-88. After six years with the company, he realised ballet was not fulfilling his dreams and left to dance with companies such as Michael Clark and DV8, while at the same time training in styles such as the Brazilian capoeira, and t'ai chi. While working with the radical improvisational dancer, Laurie Booth, he met the lighting designer, Michael Hulls, his consistent and most significant collaborator from that point onwards. By the time they encountered Guillem, they had been working together for 15 years and Maliphant had formed his own company. He was also 42 and had just decided to give up dancing in order to concentrate on choreography. So he hesitated before he agreed to Guillem's request to perform with her. "I thought it would be better if she did it with someone else," he said. "But she was very persistent so I said, 'OK, let's go into the studio together and see how we fit.'"

They began work in the South of France and continued in studios at The Place (where Hulls and Maliphant began to experiment with lighting) and at the Royal Opera House as well as at Sadler's Wells. It was a period of discovery, and "it was really, really pleasant," Guillem said. Over a total of about eight weeks of rehearsal, they explored movement, watching each other in the mirror, lying on the floor with their eyes closed, improvising blindfolded. They filmed the results, keeping the best, ruthlessly discarding anything that did not work. Maliphant would take a movement – Guillem's ability to do tango flicks where she could reach his waist with

Right: Sylvie Guillem, Michael Nunn and William Trevitt in *Broken Fall*

her leg, for example – and then try to make something of it. Or they would create a duet where they could not move their feet, and examine what they had discovered. Intense periods of creation were followed by time apart, so that Maliphant could absorb and consider what they had made.

One of the inspirations for the duet that became *Push* was a book Maliphant had been reading called *The Baron in The Trees* by Italo Calvino, a fantasy in which a child takes to life in the forest branches. As a result, he wanted to keep Guillem airborne, contrasting her light, balletic aesthetic with his own more earthbound quality. "I wanted to start with a seven-minute section of Sylvie not coming down to earth, but inevitably when we started to move around there came a point where, after a minute or two, I couldn't hold her up any more, so we had to roll apart and start again." It was Hulls's suggestion to use blackouts to disguise the effort, enabling Maliphant to lift Guillem in the semi-darkness, so when the light rose she was aloft once more. Together they created the magical opening, the stage delineated by a horizontal band of light, Guillem unwinding across Maliphant's body from a point high on his shoulders, wrapping herself around him, across his back, around his knees, each fragment of movement broken by darkness. Everything in the duet developed to complement and expand that initial sequence.

In creative terms, it was not this complex duet that caused the difficulties, but the solo that was due to open the bill. Maliphant constantly changes his pieces even after their premieres, searching for elusive perfection. With *Solo*, to a flamenco soundtrack played by Carlos Montoya, the alterations went on right up until the opening night. Part of the problem was that a commissioned score did not suit the piece, and by the time he recognised that and reverted to the Montoya recording they had used in rehearsal, the steps were still in flux. For Guillem, opening the show under a bank of bright, hot lights, it was a nightmare. "It was one of the only times I wanted to get out of the theatre before the show," she said. "I didn't know the steps in my body because it was still changing."

The premiere on September 30 2005 had cut-price standing room at the front of the auditorium, so when the door opened, the audience charged in. "I was back stage trying to memorise and concentrate on the solo. When I heard those people running in, that was the moment I said to myself, 'OK, I will go home now'. I don't know how I found the strength to stay." Of course, when the curtain rose on the dancer in short red wig, gauzy trousers and bolero top, there was no sign either of nerves or insecurity in the way she bent and turned, sharp feet flicking and flexing to the guitar's rhythm. It was the first of three astonishing solos. The second was Maliphant accompanied by three shadows of himself in *Shift*, the third Guillem again, mesmeric in the propulsive *Two*, her arms whirring through bars of light, so that she seemed to leave a trail hanging in the air behind her.

Hulls has a gift for gilding dance, shaping it like sculpture, and it was partly his lighting that cast the evening in a golden glow. But it was also the poetry of what was unfolding on stage. "When geniuses collide, sparks fly," I wrote.[8] In the duet, to Andy Cowton's elegiac score, the two dancers, almost the same height, moved around the stage with a watchful grace, their bodies in constant dialogue. What the choreography captured was not just the precision of Guillem's movement, but also its passion. Watching in the auditorium, Michael Hulls "felt

Left: Sylvie Guillem and Russell Maliphant in *Push*

a great fat tear roll down my face. It was as if something had gone straight into my chest." Debra Craine wrote in *The Times*: "It's one of the classiest nights of contemporary dance I have seen…Maliphant's choreography has never felt so emotional; Guillem has never looked lovelier."[9]

Push, which represented the first time that two dancers had held the main stage at Sadler's Wells for a complete evening, was an instant success. Seven years after that ecstatic opening, it had been performed in 17 countries and seen by more than 140,000 people. Over the years, it has changed as the dancers have come to know it so well that they can take different risks with it; it remains one of the most beautiful pieces Guillem has ever performed.

By the time it returned to Sadler's Wells the following season, it was joined in the repertory by *Sacred Monsters*, a 75-minute blend of dance, music and spoken reminiscence Guillem had made with Akram Khan. It took her into more uncharted territory. "I really think I am someone masochistic, mentally and physically," she said, with some humour, as she described the challenges of placing her ballet-trained classicism next to Khan's equally precise training in the Kathak tradition. "I want to try everything,…it is very scary, but I learnt not to be afraid of being afraid."[10] The result was another stimulating evening in which the two dancers tested each other's prowess and embarked on a dissection of the way that they viewed the art which had made them famous. Guillem revealed a musical voice and wry timing; in their inventive duets together they created images where their two dance languages appeared to merge. At one point Guillem wrapped her long legs round Khan's waist and they performed a constantly changing mirror dance. By turns funny and tender, it was another magical work.

Like *Push*, *Sacred Monsters* has revealed itself as a durable work, with the depth and resonance to allow for repeated viewings. Until 2012, when Khan suffered an injury, it was still being performed around the world.

That autumn of 2006 was notable for two things: Guillem became an associate artist, joining Maliphant who had been appointed halfway through the previous year. (Hulls followed in 2010, the first non-dancing associate.) The season also set a box office record, thanks in part to Guillem. This great dancer had brought her audience with her, people who were willing to follow her to the ends of the earth, let alone to north London. But she brought a sprinkling of stardust too. "She changed the game a bit," said Spalding. Her relationship with the theatre was not based in sentiment; its history had less meaning for her than for some of the British-born dance-makers. But she responded to the way it allowed her to go exploring. "It was exactly what I was looking for. Each time I came up with a suggestion, Alistair said yes. It is incredible – and rare."

Guillem's next suggestion was even more audacious. She had always wanted to work with the French-Canadian theatre director Robert Lepage and invited him to collaborate with her and Maliphant. Together they created *Eonnagata*, an elaborate, episodic exploration of the life of the French spy and diplomat, the Chevalier d'Eon, who lived half his life as a woman and half as a man. It featured Guillem and Maliphant speaking, and Lepage dancing; the legendary fashion designer, Alexander McQueen, contributed rich costumes without a fee in order to be part of the project. Working with a lighting budget of a kind he had not had before, Hulls helped to make the action unfolding on stage look spectacularly beautiful and some of the tableaux were

strikingly effective: a scene where Guillem flung herself across a table, writing a letter of bitter frustration; one where she and Maliphant morphed out of different sides of a mirror representing the Chevalier's two personalities. But as a theatrical experience, its premiere on March 2 2009 was a disappointment. Judith Mackrell's judgement was one of the kinder ones delivered: "While parts of the production are startlingly beautiful, touching and brave...*Eonnagata* feels like a work in progress, whose character has not yet come into focus."[11]

In fact, that was exactly what it was. Lepage had likened the process of working on the piece to a three-legged stool where each leg had to be equal.[12] What Guillem and Maliphant had not anticipated was the way in which Lepage put something on stage which was still evolving. When it opened at Sadler's Wells, it was full of ideas but lacking a sound construction. "We had all the tools, but we had not built it properly," noted Guillem. Yet as *Eonnagata* has toured, it has changed, becoming more and more successful. "It was a fantastic experience," said Guillem. "I would do it again. Once we found the stability and got rid of the obstacles, it was possible to go where we wanted to go." Maliphant too felt enriched by the experience. "It had an impact on the ways I thought about creativity and exploring things and performance." In this way, *Eonnagata* informed the works he went on to make for Sadler's Wells.

For Guillem, it became another piece that gave her new scope for her enduring gifts after she left The Royal Ballet, without fanfare, in 2007. In 2011, the year she revealed that she could still dazzle in the classics by performing Kenneth MacMillan's *Manon* at La Scala, Milan, she also commissioned two new pieces to add to her personal repertory and performed them in a double

Left: Sylvie Guillem in Mats Ek's *Bye*

bill at Sadler's Wells in July. *Bye*, choreographed by Mats Ek, was a dramatic solo in which Guillem seemed to be playing a woman who was saying farewell to her past, perhaps to freedom. *Rearray*, by William Forsythe, was something else. Created on Guillem and Nicolas Le Riche, also trained at the historic Paris Opera Ballet, it took as its starting point the classical purity which informs everything she has danced – however far she travels from it – and then subverted and explored it. "These are dancers engaged in an intricate exploration of their own art," I wrote, "examining its mysterious possibilities with love and dedication…At the end, they vanish into the darkness, still moving, in a dance that will go on for ever."[13]

Rearray provided Guillem with a summation of the voyage of discovery she has been on throughout her career. As in *Push*, that image of a great dancer, moving through space and light, endlessly searching, has been one of the glories she brought to Sadler's Wells.

Above: Sylvie Guillem and Nicolas Le Riche in William Forsythe's *Rearray*

4

SADLER'S WELLS
AND THE WORLD

To celebrate the arrival of the Olympic and Paralympic Games in London in 2012, Britain launched a huge cultural festival, full of fireworks, orchestras, new plays and public art. At its heart was an epic undertaking from Tanztheater Wuppertal Pina Bausch, who brought to the stages of Sadler's Wells and the Barbican ten huge works, each inspired by a different city.

The season, which lasted just under five weeks, began at Sadler's Wells with *Viktor,* prompted by memories of Rome, made in 1986. It takes place in a deep earthworks where the dancers perform as if in a grave, with soil periodically raining down upon them. There is hardly any actual dance, just a few stylised sequences that unfold in great swathes of movement. The stage is full of images, some disturbing (a woman in a red dress without arms, smiling at the audience), some comic (three slovenly waitresses slouching towards their customer), some sublime (women swinging high above the stalls on gymnastic rings, their long evening gowns floating in the air). The piece reeks of Rome, yet it is also universal: the whole of human life is there but, as I wrote in my review, "not so much *La Dolce Vita*, but *La Vita Amara*, full of bitter pain as well as beauty."[1]

The run ended with *Wiesenland*, made in 2000, different in mood but just as rich in imagery, danced in and around a living meadow, with water dripping down, full of lingering solos heavy with longing, and group gatherings that celebrate living. Between the two pieces, audiences saw the final work Bausch made, … *como el musguito en la piedra. ay si, si, si…* , premiered in June 2009, the month she died. Yet it isn't just that retrospective knowledge that gives the piece its haunting elegiac tone. Danced within designer Peter Pabst's black box on a smooth, white floor that intermittently cracks

Above: Pina Bausch's *Rite of Spring*

to reveal chasms beneath, it seems to encompass both the dark history of Chile and the transience of life in scenes in which couples try desperately to hold on to each other but are pulled repeatedly apart.

The entire season was a revelation. Not everybody loved it. Clement Crisp, a long-standing sceptic about Bausch wrote a declamatory review of *Viktor* which ended: "*Viktor* drones on, using up – like every major bore – all the air in the world. Breathe freely. Avoid Tanztheater."[2] Few took his advice: enthusiasts queued round the block, buying tickets for the sold-out shows on eBay in order to see as many of the works as they could; the voices in the lobbies were excited and excitable; people travelled from all over the world to be part of something unique. Sadler's Wells was suddenly the centre of the dance world. What was more, it felt like a European dance house.

This is, in itself, quite a turnaround. In the broadest terms, contemporary dance in Britain from the 1960s onwards was an American-influenced form. Robert Cohan brought Graham technique to London Contemporary Dance and when Rambert made the switch from being a ballet company to a dance company, it did so under the aegis of Norman Morrice, a man who had studied in the US with Martha Graham and others. The choreographers invited to mount work were Americans, too: Glen Tetley, Merce Cunningham, Dan Wagoner. Under Robert North and the Cunningham-influenced Richard Alston that trans-Atlantic tendency continued.

The same was true of visiting companies. Paul Taylor, Cunningham, Alvin Ailey, Graham herself. The Americans dominated the landscape, with only occasional visits from the likes of Maurice Béjart, Roland Petit (both heavily ballet-based) and Nederlands Dans Theater to indicate that something different and equally interesting was happening on the continent. By 1982, Pina Bausch was feted in Paris and Germany but when she came to London she played to half-empty halls. Lloyd Newson, who founded DV8, was one of those inspired by what he saw, yet he remembered: "swathes of audience members walking out and many critics sullenly dismissing her work as 'not dance', 'structureless' or 'self-indulgent'."[3]

Although the Edinburgh Festival kept the Bausch flame alight in Britain, her company didn't return to London until January 1999 when they first brought *Viktor* to the opening season at the rebuilt Sadler's Wells. London audiences, deprived for so long, finally had a chance to see the purveyors of the most important and influential dance theatre of our time – and to see what all the fuss was about.

From that point onwards, Tanztheater Wuppertal became regular visitors to Sadler's Wells, letting people systematically catch up. In February 2005 the company brought two immense works which tested the theatre's technical department to the limit: *Nelken* (1982), which calls for a stage covered in plastic carnations, and *Palermo Palermo* (1989), which opens with a breeze block wall crashing to the floor, filling the stage with debris and the air with choking red dust. Two more defining pieces arrived in 2008 with a double bill of the *Rite of Spring* from 1975 and *Café Müller*, made three years later.

Many agreed that Bausch's *Rite*, with its 32 dancers moving convulsively in inexorable tribal ritual across an earth-strewn stage, is a masterpiece, perhaps the best choreography of the many versions set to Stravinsky's music. But others were haunted by the dream-like sadness of *Café Müller*, full of moments that suggest meaning but are ultimately unfathomable. "It is a work,"

I wrote, "that reveals Bausch's unique gift…her ability to find images for the mystery of life."[4] Bausch, billed to dance the role of the sleepwalker on the opening night, failed to appear; she never again appeared on the Sadler's Wells stage. When her company returned in 2010, to perform *Iphigenie Auf Tauris*, to Gluck's opera, it was without their founder: sadness at her death the previous year and uncertainty about the company's future clouded a performance which revealed a work of fierce beauty.

Simply in terms of the mantra of Sadler's Wells to bring the best in world dance to its stages, this link with one of Europe's great companies is important. But for Alistair Spalding, its significance goes far deeper. In a piece written just after Bausch's death he passionately advocated her significance. "The bottom line is that what can be broadly described as European-based dance theatre has always struggled to find acceptance

in the UK, the critics preferring on the whole the less controversial minimalism of the Americans. This is a pity, as Bausch and others who have followed in her tradition have shown the world what can be achieved in dance, and have provided new narratives to replace those of the outdated 19th-century ballets."

He went on to argue that the work being produced at Sadler's Wells by creators such as Akram Khan and Sidi Larbi Cherkaoui could not have been made without Bausch's opening up of dance – particularly her inclusion of speech. Furthermore, he said: "I believe dance theatre is one of the main reasons we are seeing the current rise in the popularity of the art form."[5]

Certainly, without Bausch the career of Jasmin Vardimon, another of the Sadler's Wells associate artists, would have been entirely different. As a 14-year-old, who had just switched to dance from gymnastics, one of her

first tasks was to replenish the battered carnations that cover the stage in *Nelken*, when Tanztheater Wuppertal visited Israel. Thereafter, whenever the company arrived, Vardimon would go to watch rehearsals and take class. It was a decisive influence when she came to make her own work, decades later. "I am sure that is the reason that my genre is more towards theatre."

Vardimon, who has been an associate of Sadler's Wells since November 2006, has quietly developed her own form of dance theatre under its wing. Born and raised on a kibbutz, she moved to London in 1997, where she found support from The Place as she formed the Jasmin Vardimon Company and started to incorporate film and other forms of visual technology into passionately argued and ferociously danced pieces which seek to examine the human condition.

Vardimon's starting point is never the steps. "I like to start from a big concept and then slowly dig in and peel the layers away and find my seed in it." As a result, each of her pieces takes on a very distinct character. *Park*, shown at the Sadler's Wells Peacock Theatre in 2005, turned the open space of its title into a fantasy land

Above: Pina Bausch's *Nelken*
Left: Pina Bausch's *Viktor*

where a stone mermaid sprang to life, a skinhead turned into a growling dog and relationships were forged and foundered. In 2007, she unveiled the text-based *Justitia*, a study of a murder from multiple points of view. In 2008, she followed this tour de force with *Yesterday*, a look back on 10 years of her company, which Sanjoy Roy described in the *Guardian* as "less a trip down memory lane, than a series of blasts from the past...The hard-hitting, attention-grabbing combination of anarchic energy with military discipline pins us in our seats."[6]

7734, her first commission for the main stage of Sadler's Wells, presented in November 2010, was an indictment of man's cruelty to man, and a direct commentary on the Holocaust. It opened with dancers exploding out of the stage, shivering and grunting amid piles of rags and tattered clothes. "As a conceit it has undeniable power and for the first third of the piece, Vardimon's choreography drives the narrative with cold, clear-eyed force," said Luke Jennings in the *Observer*. But he noted the piece's lack of structure and its "leaden, didactic text".[7]

In contrast, *Freedom*, which opened in November 2012, had less speech. Like all her works, it sprang from a long rehearsal process in which Vardimon and her dancers, many of whom have been with the company for years, read, researched and developed their ideas. Only towards the end did she create the weightless steps; the contrasting sections.

Vardimon is evangelical about developing the physical theatre tradition in Britain. When it was announced that she would be the first artistic director of the National Youth Dance Company formed at Sadler's Wells in 2012, with Arts Council support, she saw it as an opportunity to help a new generation of dancers understand the genre. "I want to open dancers' minds

Left: Jasmin Vardimon's *7734*

about their ability, so they don't feel they have any restrictions. I want them to work with voice coaches and develop their theatrical skills so that they will look at themselves as more rounded performers rather than just as bodies."

The visits of Tanztheater Wuppertal and their consequences did more than add to Britain's understanding of dance theatre. They were part of an ongoing commitment by Spalding to mount retrospective seasons which have acted as a primer for British audiences wanting to see the choreographers on the cutting edge of pioneering dance. It was as if having been cut off from developments in the European avant-garde, Sadler's Wells was suddenly an integral part of it. As the London home of companies such as Tanztheater

Wuppertal, The Forsythe Company and Anne Teresa De Keersmaeker's Rosas, it has had a significant effect on British dance tastes.

This was particularly true of William Forsythe, arguably the most important post-balletic choreographer, a man who continued the tradition established by Petipa and embellished by Balanchine and took it into completely unexpected directions. It was only in 1998, after he had been making waves in Frankfurt for 14 years with his deconstructed, post-classical classicism that his Ballett Frankfurt finally made its British debut at Sadler's Wells. His work had been glimpsed at the Royal Opera House where *In the Middle, Somewhat Elevated* and *Firstext/ Steptext* made for, and danced by, Sylvie Guillem had brought a blast of modernism into the repertoire. But

Above: Anne Teresa De Keersmaeker's *Rosas danst Rosas*
Right: William Forsythe's *Three Atmospheric Studies*

Forsythe's hopes of being invited to showcase his own company had gone unrealised.

In that context, the programme he brought to Sadler's Wells as the climax of Dance Umbrella was a bold update on where his thinking was leading him. The style was still what Ismene Brown described irreverently as "hip-crackin, high-kickin, wrist-wrenchin, cool stalkin", [8] but the attention demanded by an invigorating programme which contained *Hypothetical Stream 2*, *Enemy in the Figure* and *Quintett* was of a different order. It showed Forsythe on a journey that went so far from his ballet roots that it was often unrecognisable as ballet. Forsythe cared about the reaction. "I know London. It mattered," he said. "I was shaking, I was so nervous." The Royal Ballet principal Leanne Benjamin was sitting in front of him as his performers went through fiercely calibrated movements. "She watched for a bit and then turned around to me and said 'I feel so lazy', which was very sweet."

Five renegades who just had resigned from The Royal Ballet to form a company with Tetsuya Kumakawa were also in the stalls, catching up on the kind of dance that London had been missing for so long. Amongst them were Michael Nunn and William Trevitt, soon to become the BalletBoyz – key motivators in the slow moving of tectonic plates that was changing the dance world. Spalding at this point was still at the Southbank Centre. When he saw the work of William Forsythe

on the Sadler's Wells stage, he at once recognised the potential, so that when he took over as the director of programming in 2000 he was determined to pursue the vision that the theatre had revealed in that first season. "I had the idea you could make it more contemporary."

By the time Spalding moved to north London the money which facilitated such adventurous planning had run out and the theatre had to make a surplus of £30,000 a week in order to keep its financial head above water. But with some judicious juggling, Spalding managed to bring Ballett Frankfurt back with two programmes in 2001: *Artifact*, Forsythe's 1984 ode to ballet itself, and *Eidos:Telos*, an exhilarating three-act meditation on death, myth, time and space. In the season programme Spalding said: "When I first saw *Eidos:Telos* it was a moment when my view of what was possible in dance was totally overturned."

Forsythe, now working with the smaller and more experimental Forsythe Company, soon became a regular visitor. By 2006, London saw *Three Atmospheric Studies* on stage at Sadler's Wells just six months after it had premiered at the Berlin Theatre Festival. In Germany the debate had been whether this explosive, angry piece, which set the Iraq war alongside Cranach's *Crucifixion*, the pity of war with the history of art, could really be called theatre; in Britain, the argument was whether it could be called dance. In the *Telegraph*, I wrote: "What I love about William Forsythe is his belief that dance can do anything."[9] What was clear to everyone, whether they loved or disliked the piece, was just how far Forsythe had moved from anyone's notion of the traditional dance-maker.

Two years later, Sadler's Wells marked Forsythe's 60th birthday with a revealing look back. In 2008, classical companies such as the Mariinsky and Royal Ballet of Flanders presented his early pieces, fractured and distorted and full of alien disruptions, but clearly rooted in the classical lineage. Then, in 2009, the almost three-week long season, *Focus on Forsythe*, explained his new incarnation as something close to a conceptual artist in exhibitions and installations that spread out from Sadler's Wells and appeared across London. Most memorable was *You made me a monster*, a searingly humane installation in which the audience builds models of a body while the dancers slowly reveal the story of a death. Most luminous was *Nowhere and Everywhere at the Same Time*, in which the company danced among pendulums in the Turbine Hall at Tate Modern.

For the choreographer, it was an extraordinary tribute, a sign of his growing closeness to a theatre that has been willing to follow him down every tributary of exploration. "Alistair is really interested in the conversation you are having," he said. "He is a champion of the work, as opposed to someone who is just buying a tour. As far as I am concerned, every city in the world needs a Sadler's Wells."

As far as Anne Teresa De Keersmaeker is concerned, the experience of establishing a relationship with Sadler's Wells has been equally rewarding. Its programme, she said, is unlike anything in Europe, since it combines popular entertainment with much more experimental and demanding works such as those created by her company Rosas. Yet as she has returned again and again over the years, the relationship she has built with a British audience has been "crucial". "You feel that people get a deeper insight into the work by seeing all these different works," she said. De Keersmaeker divides dance opinion even more strongly than Bausch or Forsythe, which

Right: William Forsythe's *Nowhere and Everywhere at the Same Time* at Tate Modern

means that she recognises just how bold it was for Sadler's Wells continually to promote her work on its main stage. "The pressure on large theatres to make spectacular work is huge, so it is very good to choose to present challenging work."

Her rigorous, repetitive creations will never suit all tastes. In 2009, the ground-breaking *Rosas danst Rosas* – a 100-minute marathon of repetitive movement for four women – infuriated and impressed people just as much as it had done in 1983, but its cultural significance was heavily underlined afterwards when Beyoncé seemed to borrow some of its moves for a – considerably shorter – pop video. By the time Rosas returned to present four early works over six days in 2011, Debra Craine could write of *Fase* "it is a work of bewitching complexity and dazzling accuracy that lays bare the essence of movement."[10]

The advantage of persistent exposure was that audiences – critics included – had a chance to make up their minds, judging and enjoying each piece on its merits. I was transfixed by *3Abschied*, De Keersmaeker and Jérôme Bel's strange examination of the effects of Mahler's famous farewell from *The Song of the Earth*, which arrived at Sadler's Wells in November 2011. "It is pretentious, annoying and long. But it is also strangely compelling," I wrote in the *Telegraph*.[11] Judith Flanders of the Arts Desk had a similarly split reaction to the next two pieces Rosas staged at the theatre: *En Atendant* and *Cesena*, a diptych in which one work travels from dawn to dusk and the other progresses in the opposite direction. She said, "As always with De Keersmaeker, [the opening] goes on for longer than seems entirely sane, and yet, also as always, you come out the other side feeling altered, stripped back."[12] Some people walked out. But

those who stayed were confronted with creations of stark beauty and rigorous thought.

These two works marked De Keersmaeker's second visit to London in 2012. Her first was to open the Tate Tanks, a new gallery space at Tate Modern devoted to live art, with a staging of *Fase*. Like the Forsythe season before it, this was part of a trend set by Sadler's Wells: by presenting choreographers as artists, the theatre helped dance to break the bounds of the stage and enter the general cultural debate.

Yet the traffic in thought-provoking dance has not been one way. When Alistair Spalding first announced his new commissioning policy he said: "As well as just receiving international work, which is great for London audiences, we want to put something back. Hopefully these productions will go around the world."[13] That wish has been fulfilled. The theatre has forged links with theatres all over the globe: from Singapore, Wellington and Sydney, to Bucharest, Berlin, Milan and Madrid, there is hardly a city that has not seen the works it commissioned from choreographers such as Wayne McGregor, Russell Maliphant, Akram Khan and Hofesh Shechter. Pieces such as *Push*, *zero degrees*, *Sacred Monsters*, *Eonnagata* and *Entity* have toured extensively. It is not only reputations that are enhanced; international touring also enables these companies and choreographers to thrive financially. "It has a big economic impact on what we do," Wayne McGregor said. "If I only did national touring, even with Arts Council support, I'd be going nowhere."

It is a virtuous circle: good, interesting, challenging art imported from around the world – and good, interesting, challenging art exported once more. Sadler's Wells and its associates are now major players in world dance.

5

MATTHEW BOURNE AND WELCOMING AN AUDIENCE

In the summer of 2011, the choreographer Matthew Bourne reached a decision. On a visit to Russia, he went to Tchaikovsky's house and found himself sitting in the composer's bedroom, next to his writing desk. "I thought, this is a sign. That was the day I decided to stage *The Sleeping Beauty*."

The production, which opened at Sadler's Wells in December 2012, celebrated Bourne's extraordinary 25 years in charge of his own company New Adventures, a period which had seen him become both the most commercially successful and the best-known choreographer in Britain.

He has negotiated an array of obstacles to end up in such a pre-eminent position. He only started formal dance training at the age of 22 when, inspired by a love of Fred Astaire and Frederick Ashton, he decided to audition for a course in Dance Theatre at the Laban Centre; his adolescent passions were musicals and autograph hunting rather than the refined esoteric world of classical ballet. But exactly that difference of viewpoint meant that when Bourne turned his attention to the traditional ballet repertoire, he brought a refreshingly original approach along with him.

He started on a small scale with some original works such as *Spitfire*, made in 1988, which turned Perrot's famous *Pas de Quatre*, made as a calling card for four great romantic ballerinas, into an underwear advertisement for four preening men. When this tiny piece was revived at Sadler's Wells as part of the anniversary celebrations, I noticed that "all the hallmarks of his later successes are there: a clever, irreverent wit, a new way of looking at things, an affection for dance, a desire to entertain and provoke."[1]

Left: Matthew Bourne's *Sleeping Beauty*

Those successes included *Highland Fling*, which transposed the 19th-century romanticism of the classical *La Sylphide* into a Glasgow tenement and turned the flighty fairy into a zombie-like hallucination, and an equally radical rethinking of *The Nutcracker*, set in a brutal orphanage and a multi-coloured place called Sweetieland, a ballet that was his first at Sadler's Wells.

But it was in 1995 that Bourne made the breakthrough that transformed his fortunes. When he announced that he was planning to stage at Sadler's Wells a version of *Swan Lake* that would use the Tchaikovsky score but would feature a dysfunctional Royal family, an emotionally crippled Prince who hates his mother, and a chorus of bare-chested male swans led by former Royal Ballet star Adam Cooper, as a male Odette, people feared that the entire thing would be a send-up. Bourne's response was clear: "This is a tragedy and I'm not spending nearly three hours sending it up. That would be a bit over the top don't you think?"[2] He was, however, really nervous about the size of the task. *Swan Lake* was a leap of faith for everyone – the Arts Council, the theatre, all its financial backers. "We all felt it was a good idea and were determined to make it work," he said. "But that's different from being confident." He needn't have worried; by the interval at the opening on November 14, Cameron Mackintosh suggested that the show should transfer to the West

Above and right: Matthew Bourne's *Swan Lake*

End. By the close, the audience were rapturous – and even the critics, while expressing some reservations, knew that they were witnessing a new dawn. "One of the most gripping, funny and profoundly moving dance works I've seen," wrote Judith Mackrell.[3]

The rest really is dance history. Bourne had said that "if all goes well on opening night, it will be as good as winning the lottery."[4] His *Swan Lake* did indeed turn itself into the equivalent of a lottery win, becoming over the next two years the longest-running ballet in the West End, triumphing on Broadway, and winning numerous awards. Adapted and refined by Bourne, it is still touring the world, and still celebrated. In 1996 it felt even more like a good deed in a dirty world: dance in Britain generally was firmly in the doldrums.

This was the year that the weak position of The Royal Ballet within the Royal Opera House was exposed in the fly-on-the-wall television documentary *The House*; the year too that Siobhan Davies had to choose between paying her dancers an extra £50 a week, or making a new work. Bourne's own company, before *Swan Lake*, was grateful for a grant from the National Lottery that enabled it to buy a computer system and a photocopier. As Nigel Reynolds said in the *Daily Telegraph*, in this context, the way *Swan Lake* "put the sex and the spectacular back into ballet"[5] seemed little short of miraculous.

It was the last success Sadler's Wells enjoyed before the old theatre was torn down and rebuilding began. As a man who loved the history of his craft, Bourne had always liked working in the old building, rehearsing in the rooms where Margot Fonteyn had once stood at the barre, and – when he danced the part of the Knickerbocker Glory in *The Nutcracker* – performing on the stage where de Valois had launched her company. When Spalding arrived in

Sadler's Wells as the director of programming, he knew that Bourne was one of the choreographers he had to entice back. The two men had first met in Crawley, when Spalding collected Bourne from the station in a battered Vauxhall Viva and drove him off to run dance workshops. Although much had changed, one thing remained constant: Bourne's ability to create entertaining dance narratives that audiences wanted to see. "For me one of the key moments was bringing Matthew back," said Spalding. "He has been crucial to both the artistic and economic well-being of the house."

The first Bourne production at the new Sadler's Wells was a much-revised *Nutcracker*. Announcing its arrival in the season's brochure, the then chief executive Ian Albery claimed that it would be "the most-talked about 'must-see' show this Christmas". Originally booked for eight weeks, it proved so popular that it ran for 12. The following Christmas, it returned for another six-week run. In 2004, *Swan Lake* returned for a six-week post-Christmas run, which played once again to packed and enthusiastic houses. Bourne's unique combination of popularity and creative curiosity make him a theatre manager's dream, but the relationship between Bourne and the theatre would not have thrived if Bourne's artistic ambitions had not been allowed scope to grow.

Given this, *Edward Scissorhands* which premiered amid much fanfare on November 30 2005 was an important project. Bourne had wanted to turn Tim Burton's movie into dance for almost eight years: its appeal for him originally lay in Danny Elfman's score – though in the end Elfman was too busy to compose the stage version, and the ballet ended up with music based on Elfman's score, written by Terry Davies. He was also inspired, however, by the idea of making a ballet that was

Above and right: Matthew Bourne's *Edward Scissorhands*

Above: Matthew Bourne's *Nutcracker!*

based on something that had been popular in a different arena, working with a title that appealed to people who might never have seen dance before. "Titles are still very important in dance and if you do something people have never heard of, there is no guarantee they will come."

The obvious problem with choreographing a piece about a boy with inflexible scissors for hands is that the hands cannot be made to dance. But this for Bourne was part of the appeal. "Restrictions, problems, things to overcome, limitations. Those are always good to address at the outset. Because then you have to try to make them work."[6]

He saw Edward as the ultimate outsider, and to make that alienation clear he had not only to create a convincing central figure, without the benefit of Johnny Depp's achingly sorrowful close-ups, but also to people the stage as vividly as he could with the society that ultimately rejects him. With the help of his regular designer Lez Brotherston's colourful, skewed 1950s designs and a generous production budget of some £1.3 million, he poured into *Scissorhands* some of his most lively and inventive ideas.

By the end, when snow fell on the audience, they were on their feet cheering. This direct bond between Bourne and his audience is one of the most enduring in dance. He brings people to Sadler's Wells and theatres around the world, who would never dream of buying a ticket for "contemporary dance". Yet he is a contemporary dance-maker who tells his stories entirely through the medium of choreography; unlike Akram Khan, for example, he never uses words or a script.

Certainly, the reaction to *Scissorhands* was astonishing. It ran for 11 weeks – a record beaten only by Bourne's own *Nutcracker!* – and of the 95,000 people who came

to see it, 65 per cent were coming to Sadler's Wells for the first time. 20 per cent of those debutants went on to book another show at the theatre. The piece then toured almost constantly in Britain, Europe and across America until the end of 2009, with Bourne making changes and improvements as it went. By the time it returned to Sadler's Wells for another seven weeks in 2009 it was clearer and better.

Critics worry about Bourne's lack of choreographic complexity, but people respond to his directness, and his showman's ability to create stage pictures that speak louder than words. In *Nutcracker!*, they love the Gobstoppers, who are clearly loutish boys on the make, and the Marshmallow Girls, bright ladies on a hen night, high heels flicking outwards, feathered hats bobbing in time to the music. In *Swan Lake*, they laugh at the corgis, or the dark stranger seducing the imperious Queen, but they also respond to the swans, emerging from a park lake in the night, full of the otherness of everything we do not understand. The basis of Bourne's success lies in his imaginative incisiveness.

He required all of that quality, plus a fair dash of audacity, when it came to staging *The Sleeping Beauty*. He had been running away from the idea for years, unable to think of "a good enough idea or an idea that worked for me." But once he had decided to complete his Tchaikovsky trilogy, he went to his house by the sea for 10 weeks to listen to the music and think. He watched as many versions of the ballet as he could find, and read widely, studying everything from psychoanalytic studies of why teenagers sleep so much (they don't want to grow up) to the origins of fairy stories. He also, characteristically, noted the way Walt Disney had strengthened the love story in his popular cartoon version of the tale.

Slowly, he realised that if he wanted Aurora to wake up in the present day, he could create a timeline where she fell asleep in 1911, the golden summer of the Edwardian age. That meant that he could set the first part of the story in 1890, the year Petipa and Tchaikovsky premiered the work. Then he began to shape a story quite different from the usual telling, one which featured vampires, avenging sons, a childhood sweetheart and a male Count Lilac.

His method for actually turning such scenarios into dance is idiosyncratic. For Beauty, he gathered a small group of trusted dancers and collaborators together for two workshops. Bourne provided ideas he wanted to explore, a detailed scenario and some research he thought would prompt creative thinking. He asked the dancers to learn the original Petipa fairy variations so they understood them before making their own; they watched Edwardian social dancing; they created a party sequence

based on their Zodiac signs. The result was 200 snippets of filmed movement which provided the basis for the next stage.

Etta Murfitt, who has been with New Adventures since its foundation, explained: "Matt is really good at giving a task and saying 'this is what I want. This is what I am feeling.' And then you have a go at doing it and he takes the best bits and puts them together." This process is more akin to editing than to conventional choreography. "I can't do anything with nothing, which is why I don't take commissions," Bourne said. "Once something is there I will hone away at it for ever and keep thinking about exactly what it will be. What I think I am most good at is setting the material to music. I want to honour the music and I use it in quite a detailed way."[7]

He remains almost preternaturally calm throughout the process, cracking jokes and preserving an air of

Above: Matthew Bourne's *Dorian Gray*
Right: Matthew Bourne's *Nutcracker!*

detachment even when all around him are displaying signs of anxiety. However, it would be a mistake to read such serenity for a lack of authority: he knows what he wants and intervenes constantly to show exactly the placing of the arms and head, or the right level of energy, or the narrative clarity that he always seeks. "The only pressure I feel is the pressure to deliver a good show. I really want to deliver something that people like. I want it to be as good as it can be."[8]

The resulting production, with richly detailed designs by Brotherston, was sumptuous, smart and radical. It opened with a puppet Princess Aurora, who is clearly from birth her own girl, crawling away from her adoring parents, climbing the curtains with rebellious glee, sitting up in bed

to look at the fairies who entered on a moving walkway to bequeath their gifts to her. With his tomboyish heroine centre stage from the start, Bourne once more conjured a kind of narrative magic. His bold strokes – choreographing a love duet to the famous strains of the Rose Adagio, giving the bad fairy Carabosse a charismatic son, rethinking Aurora's century-long sleep as a kind of limbo which ends in the present day – gave the music and the story vivid and satisfying new life. "In Bourne's clever gothic rewrite, he has triumphantly discovered something beguiling and true," said Judith Mackrell.[9]

Sleeping Beauty opened at Sadler's Wells on December 7, 2012, and stayed there until the end of January, filling the theatre with Bourne's special brand of Christmas

delight. *New York Times* dance critic Alastair Macaulay, who collaborated with Bourne on a series of biographical interviews, has suggested that part of the choreographer's value to Sadler's Wells is this warmth. Into a theatre that is deliberately plain and monochrome, Bourne consistently brings colour and life. Bourne himself acknowledged that he tries, with each production, to welcome the audience in. "I think dance can have a cold atmosphere when you arrive, there is a lot of silence and being on your best behaviour, and I try to break that down."

It is a quality that chimes with Spalding's mission to democratise dance. Talking to *The Times* in 2010, he said that Bourne was a perfect fit with the identity he wanted to give to Sadler's Wells. "He provides a way into the art form."[10] Bourne in turn is proud of the change that he has played a part in bringing about. It was entirely appropriate that the film of *Billy Elliot*, a celebration of the power of dance, ended with an image from Bourne's *Swan Lake*. "There are guys who saw my *Swan Lake* as kids and they could suddenly see themselves doing that. Maybe it's given people a new love in their lives, of music and dance."[11]

If this far-reaching appeal is one part of the explanation for the close relationship between Sadler's Wells and Bourne, the financial security provided on both sides is the other half of the equation. Bourne's company is protected from making a loss on its seasons; but it shares its profits generously with the theatre. For its part, Sadler's Wells repays that bounty, by providing Bourne with a base – he has an office in what was once the box office on the opposite side of the road – and a springboard from which to make new work and develop older pieces.

For example, Spalding prompted the choreographer to look again at his *Cinderella*, set in wartime London and thus perfect for a 2010 revival to mark the 75th anniversary of the Blitz. Less immediately approachable than either *The Nutcracker* or *Swan Lake*, it was first premiered in the West End and suffered by comparison with its two illustrious predecessors. Reworked in December 2010 it emerged as a deeply felt personal work, full of true love and human sympathy. It also, as I said in my review, captured perfectly "the furtive, febrile atmosphere of wartime London where time is running out, kisses are stolen, drinks snatched and life sucked up in its giddy abandon."[12]

For all his popular success, however, Bourne has persisted in his desire to make work that pushes his own artistic boundaries, anxious to explore different and more difficult territory as well. When he said he wanted to make a strongly sexual and dark version of Oscar Wilde's *The Picture of Dorian Gray*, the theatre supported his ambition, backing a ballet that marked a new direction.

At root, the relationship between Bourne and Sadler's Wells can best be explained by the fact that his desire to create dance that is directly approachable is served by a theatre that prides itself on its transparency and inclusivity. Without the presence of this instinctive populariser, Sadler's Wells could still have presented some of the best in European and British contemporary dance. But it would not have been loved in the same way.

For Bourne, the process was a pleasure. He enjoys being one of a group of richly contrasting associate artists, feeling part of the bigger purpose of the development of dance. But in the end his feelings about his association with the theatre are quite simple. "Sadler's Wells is home. That's one of the reasons I love it. I feel I've come home."

6

WAYNE MCGREGOR AND THE SCIENCE OF DANCE

A group of dancers is on an uncluttered stage, bathed in rich golden light. They snap and stretch their limbs into sleek, hyper-extended distortions. Their bottoms stick out, their arms curl upwards like corkscrews, seeming to rotate both in and out simultaneously, every part of their bodies is first articulated and then takes an unexpected direction. In the same moment, they look both stunningly beautiful and startlingly alien. It is, unmistakably, a work by Wayne McGregor.

By 2012, McGregor was arguably the most talked about contemporary choreographer in Britain, awarded a CBE for his services to dance not only at Sadler's Wells, but also at the Royal Opera House, where he had been resident choreographer since 2006. He had made works for the Paris Opera Ballet, New York City Ballet, Nederlands Dans Theater, San Francisco, Australian and Stuttgart Ballets. He had even choreographed the dance scenes for a blockbusting film, *Harry Potter and the Goblet of Fire*.

But in 1995, he was at the very start of this glorious career, another choreographer struggling to make ends meet but helped by having an office in what he now describes as "the warren" of the old Sadler's Wells. These roots that reach deep into the theatre's fabric are as strong as those that bind Matthew Bourne, and the fact that Sadler's Wells has been able to accommodate and assist these two great shapers of 21st-century dance speaks volumes about the theatre's inclusive qualities.

For if Bourne has been the heart of the house, McGregor has undoubtedly been its brain, his cool musings on cognitive theory, spatial dissociation and gender neutrality in marked contrast to Bourne's emotional and involving narratives. But each is as important as the other, fulfilling Alistair Spalding's belief that a dance house must encompass

Right: Wayne McGregor's *Amu*

Above: Wayne McGregor's *Entity*

and welcome dance in all its forms – provided it embraces excellence in every area.

Bourne and McGregor in fact come from similar backgrounds, though McGregor is ten years younger. For Bourne's close London family and autograph-hunting youth, substitute McGregor's "utterly stable, utterly normal"[1] home in Cheshire, where he was a fan of disco and the films of John Travolta. But he studied classical music as a child and his path into a career in dance started with a first class degree in the subject from Bretton Hall and jobs in community dance.

In 1992 he founded his own company, Random, and the lineaments of his style and his preoccupations began to emerge: startling movement, propulsive music, a preoccupation with new technologies, which meant he incorporated animation, digital film, and even virtual dancers into his live choreography. From the late 1990s, Spalding, then commissioning dance for London's Southbank Centre, was an advocate and supporter.

So it was inevitable that when Spalding moved to Sadler's Wells he encouraged McGregor to come with him. Random became the first resident company in the new building in 2001. It was a tumultuous time in the life of the theatre, but Spalding constantly encouraged McGregor "to take a risk at the next level" in order to develop. "When he believes in an artist he believes in the whole picture," McGregor said. "He buys into that idea that your work is in constant evolution and that what is interesting is the long term."

The results of that policy were quickly obvious on stage. McGregor's early works were characterised by his own spiky qualities as a dancer. Shaven-headed, tall and extremely flexible, he was in the words of David Jays "capable of dazzling switch and swivel".[2] In *Nemesis*,

the first creation of Random's residency, Judith Mackrell described him as "dancing his own solo voyage through space"[3] in a work that attached long, steel proboscises to the dancers' arms, turning them into subterranean creatures in a dystopian world.

At the time, Spalding said: "The programming here is always going to be diverse because you are so dependent on the audience. But I'm trying to develop the sense that Sadler's Wells is somewhere you might see something unexpected, something to surprise you."[4] That policy held as he took over the reins at the theatre, and McGregor simultaneously left the stage and pushed his company's work in ever more interesting directions.

John Ashford, former director of The Place, once said: "Wayne is the most inquisitive man I know,"[5] and it was a tribute to that constant curiosity that in 2003, he was appointed research fellow of the Department of Neuroscience at Cambridge. In *AtaXia*, premiered at Sadler's Wells the following year, he unveiled the results of six months' research, sending his dancers into spasms of apparently uncontrolled, flailing movement.

In 2005's *Amu* the heart was the organ under examination. Working with a score inspired by the composer John Tavener's own heart condition, McGregor and his dancers watched open-heart surgery (he fainted), scanned their own hearts and studied the poetry of Sufi mystics to produce a piece that tackled both the heart's emotions and workings. The hour-long work had a kind of swooning sensuality, a rich inner beauty that marked yet another development.

For McGregor this has been part of the value of his relationship with Sadler's Wells, and with Spalding in particular. It has generated a sense of belief, which has underpinned the taste for adventure that Random has been able to display. "As an artist you are always looking for people to champion you. If people give you opportunities, that is the way your work evolves."

In a profound way, McGregor fits the new Sadler's Wells. His choreographic style suits the aesthetic of the auditorium, where the shape of the proscenium arch doesn't stand between the viewers and the viewed; the feeling of the place inspires what he calls his "spirit of enquiry", his instinct to make challenging work. The crusading heritage and history of Sadler's Wells, combined with the expectations Random generates means that audiences are quickly ready to go along with his desire to experiment. "You feel totally free."

This became particularly important after 2006. McGregor's restless creative spirit had always led him to take on freelance commissions and in that year he made *Chroma* for The Royal Ballet, his second work on the main stage of the Royal Opera House. It was a sensation. Behind the headlines about "Acid House at the Opera House" and "punk in the Garden" was a real frisson at the thrilling effect of the collision of McGregor's new ways of thinking and bodies that had been ballet-trained in the traditional manner.

The then director of The Royal Ballet, Monica Mason, quickly understood the potential of inviting this radical outsider to formalise his relationship with the Royal, a company that was anxious to attract new and younger audiences. She offered, and McGregor accepted, the post of resident choreographer. At this point it would have been easy for his relationship with Sadler's Wells to end, but Spalding's "generosity of spirit", as McGregor put it, combined with clear-sightedness on all sides, meant that from that point onwards he ran these different obligations in parallel, continuing to pioneer with Random, while at the same time choreographing at Covent Garden.

Whatever he is making, watching McGregor at work in the studio is a disconcerting experience. For one thing, although music is extremely important to him – he is one of the few choreographers who can read orchestral scores – he rarely works on the steps with the eventual soundtrack playing. He fears the dancers may become bored with hearing the same themes repeated in the rehearsal rooms; he likes the way too that he can set different moods by causing contrasting pieces to accompany their work.

For another, he generates his own kind of accompaniment, swooping around the dancers with a "boom-ti-boom" or a "waah-oh" or even a "bah, prrr, um bah", as he explains the rhythmic punctuation of the steps, clicking his fingers, giving the dancers shapes to remember. When he came to make *Entity*, his next piece for Random at Sadler's Wells, premiered on April 10 2008, Alice O'Keefe was invited to report on rehearsals for the *New Statesman*. It was, she said, like "watching a beautifully synchronised set of malfunctioning robots".

She described how McGregor would call out numbers and his dancers would break off into groups, going through jagged solos and smooth, sliding duets. His commands were revealing. "This needs to be like underwater dancing." "Make it fatter." Or, most vividly: "Imagine you are a boa constrictor that has just eaten something." He also explained the way in which he worked. "I always say the research is not related to the piece. The research is one thing and the piece when it is created is something independent."[6]

The research for *Entity* was particularly dense. After two years in which he had been engaged on other projects,

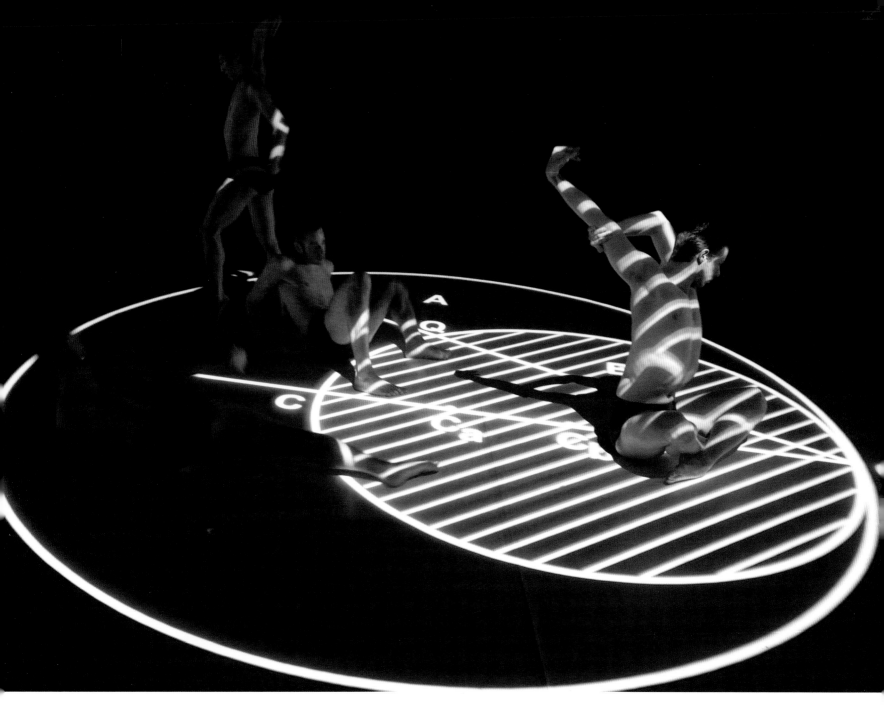

McGregor had reshaped Random, recruiting eight new dancers, four of whom were absolutely new to the process of working with him, into the ten-strong company. Once again, it was his interest in the workings of the brain that provided the backdrop to the choreography, but *Entity* sprang specifically from his involvement with a three-year "choreography and cognition" project which he helped to spearhead with scientists from Cambridge, San Diego and the University of Sussex.

He was interested in developing an entirely new choreographic entity, a piece of software that could help to develop movement. But his research with neuroscientists

Above: Wayne McGregor's *Entity*

also left him fascinated by the relationship between the brain and the body. His interest in dance itself made him want to explore the "otherness" that movement can communicate, the something beyond words that only dance can provoke.

The problems McGregor had with explaining all of this spilled over into an incredibly complex programme note and a baffled reaction from some critics. In a sense *Entity* made explicit something that has bedevilled his career. Despite his verbal dexterity, it is difficult to describe in words what he is doing, and the more he tries to explain, the more people search for explicit references to that exposition in the pieces he creates. Yet at his best, McGregor creates a work that has absorbed all the research and technology he has put into it, without each separate thought needing to find expression on stage.

In its Sadler's Wells premiere, *Entity* emerged not as an abstract scientific speculation but, as David Jays said in his review, as "a great sexy beast of a piece…It is like being licked by a panther's juicy, rasping tongue while you are revising maths."[7] Lit by McGregor's regular collaborator Lucy Carter, it took the form of a diptych, the first half set to a string quartet by Joby Talbot, the second to a throbbing electronic score by Jon Hopkins. Patrick Burnier's set, built to suggest a skeleton and skin, also transformed itself: the horizontal panels which initially surround the dancers, were raised in the course of the action on giant booms, so that they overhung the space like the dippers on oil rigs. On their surface, digital films were projected.

Within this space, the dancers looked as if they were specimens in an experiment and the films suggested the evolution of their own DNA codes which they carried written on their loose vests in the opening section, and

then shed for the black-clad second part. But the piece also had a beauty which defied easy analysis: the solos, duets and group dances seemed to reveal the very nature of locomotion. The movement itself was full of questions, tentative and unanswered; the mood was by turns tender, aggressive, predatory and wondering. It also featured two little kisses – a motif that recurs quietly in all McGregor's creations.

Writing in the *Observer*, the weekend after *Entity* had premiered, Luke Jennings noticed the way in which "McGregor has refined his language to an almost classical level of formalism". Tellingly too, he yoked him with Christopher Wheeldon and Matthew Bourne as the three most significant choreographers in Britain. "Of the three," he continued, "McGregor is probably the most significant in that his work unreservedly addresses the present. Not an idealised or imaginary present, but the actual data-streaming times we live in."[8]

That modernity drives McGregor onward. He is never entirely satisfied with the work he has just completed; he always wants to make something new. "I love the process of doing the next one, so the one you have just made always seems in some way wrong, or flawed or problematic." His next venture at Sadler's Wells, in 2010, was *FAR*, another scientifically-tinged 60-minutes, this time with music by Ben Frost and a set that included a computerised pin-board of more than 3,000 LED lights.

It was inspired both by further cognitive experiments into the way dancers actually learn to move, and by Roy Porter's distinguished book about the 18th-century Enlightenment, *Flesh in the Age of Reason*. Porter's observation that "the body was the inseparable dancing partner of the mind or soul – now in step, now a tangle of limbs and intentions, mixed emotions", quoted in

Right: Wayne McGregor's *Entity*

the programme, chimed with McGregor's own sense of the interlinked nature of the brain and body, and described what he presented on stage. Once again, the choreographer seemed to have refined his characteristic movement vocabulary, keeping its isolations, its unusual fluency, but at the same time conjuring images of complete originality: girls folding their bodies like jack-knives and balancing on their toes; couples nuzzling like gentle animals.

Like *Entity*, *FAR* has toured extensively round Britain and across the world. It has become not only part of McGregor's repertory, but an example of how British dance is seen: contemporary, questing, intelligent. Along with the creations of the other Sadler's Wells associates

Above and Left: Wayne McGregor's *FAR*

such as Akram Khan, Russell Maliphant, Matthew Bourne, and Hofesh Shechter, the new work flooding out of Sadler's Wells theatre has fundamentally altered the ecology of the dance network in Britain.

Broadly speaking, before Spalding began his commissioning policy, new creations in British contemporary dance were at best sporadic. Rambert Dance Company, a regular visitor to Sadler's Wells, had an exemplary record of original work; individual British artists such as Siobhan Davies, Jonathan Burrows, Lloyd Newson and Michael Clark, and those based here such as Javier De Frutos, made distinctive and influential pieces that kept the creative spirit of dance alive. But since each piece – then as now – was reliant on individual project funding from the Arts Council and other funding bodies, there was a pressure, particularly in the regions, to produce work that pleased audiences rather than stretched the boundaries of what was permissible; there was little sense of a continuing effort to promote new choreography.

That began to change when Sadler's Wells decided to encourage its choreographers over an extended period of time, to let them develop in the directions they wanted to pursue. Sometimes this is simply a question of asking its associates what they want to do next, and then supporting them – both financially and in terms of advice – while they pursue their vision. On other occasions – such as McGregor's *UNDANCE* – Spalding takes a more active role as a producer, coming up with an idea which he wants to develop.

But in both instances he is acting as an active promoter of dance, which originates at Sadler's Wells and then percolates through the British dance scene. As the theatre showcases more and more work – there were 106 shows, commissioned and imported, on its stages in 2011/12,

compared with 32, all touring, in 1999 – it encourages dance to grow by the simple expedient of providing audiences with more dance to watch.

Furthermore, because work that would once have been regarded as too difficult and abstruse for such a big venue has been shown on the Sadler's Wells stage, it has helped to alter the scope and ambition of new contemporary work. "I really do applaud the way Sadler's Wells has tried to get choreographers to be ambitious about performing on the big stage and not to remain in that ghetto of the mid-scale and small venues," said Matthew Bourne. Duets such as *zero degrees* and *Push* would once have been regarded as studio works; the fact that they could hold a stage and find an audience altered expectations. For McGregor too, this chance to extend his vision towards larger horizons resulted in big, bold choices. But he points out that this does not only benefit him; it also frees space in smaller venues for other choreographers to get their start.

The problem emerging dance makers have traditionally faced is that there are only a few commissioning spots, the Arts Council's portfolio is full of established companies, and dance begins to stagnate. According to McGregor, by opening its stage to new works, Sadler's Wells is beginning to break the logjam. "I don't think you can divorce what Sadler's Wells has been able to do with the cultural landscape of the development of British dance over the past 20 years and the ways that creators are now thinking about dance and the repertory. If the bigger institutions start to move in different directions, all of a sudden space starts to open up."

By transforming itself from a receiving house into a producing one, Sadler's Wells has effected this fundamental shift.

7

BREAKIN' CONVENTION AND THE GROWTH OF HIP HOP

On the evening of a performance, the foyers of Sadler's Wells are generally full of people queuing patiently for tickets, waiting anxiously for their friends, chatting softly in anticipation. On the first Bank Holiday weekend in May that genteel scene is disrupted. Doormen stand at the entrances, and fierce beats thud through the floors. The place is packed. Instead of standing, people are actually dancing. In the bars, in the mezzanine, in the corner by the loos, there are youngsters letting movement surge through their bodies, catching the rhythm of the music as they jut their heads and jerk their arms in the unmistakable contractions and relaxations of hip hop dance. Some of this activity is organised: experts are teaching children who in turn strut their stuff. But some of it seems to flow spontaneously from the simple pleasure of being amongst so many like-minded people; there's a desire to move, to show what you can do.

This is the mood of Breakin' Convention, held at the theatre since 2004. It transforms the place, putting graffiti (both real and virtual) on the walls, taking out half the seats in the auditorium so that people can stand as well as sit to watch the crews who perform, applauding their breaking, popping and locking with expert screams, whistles, honks and hoots of approval. The performers, after their turn is done, join the crowd, creating a vibrant spirit where viewer and dancer join in appreciation of the skills on display. Given the number of children there, the audience age is halved at a stroke; it is also racially mixed. But what has always been astonishing about Breakin' Convention is just how easily it fits into the theatre's walls. The kids simply walk in and own the place. As Clement Crisp, critic for the *Financial Times*, noticed: "Here was that ideal dance state (and one so ideal that it seemed impossible of realisation), where the watchers are as dedicated, as knowledgeable as the performers, where indeed there seems no separation between public and stage, between art and consumer."[1]

Breakin' Convention illustrates the way in which parallel impulses can collide to create something of cultural significance. Its launch was in the same year as the theatre started its equally successful Flamenco Festival. Both sprang from a realisation that the London dance audience is not a single mass but made up of many different audiences, with different interests. Since London is a world city, with various ethnic populations, reflecting that helps to build a broader audience – crucial if you are a theatre that essentially needs to make your money through the box office. "If you offer more choice, you expand the number of people who are interested in coming," Alistair Spalding said.

But this recognition, which also lay behind the creation of the Svapnagata festival of Indian-infused music and dance in 2009, runs alongside a belief that dance should be something that everybody can enjoy. In part, this springs from Spalding's own initiation, when a girlfriend took him to see Merce Cunningham at Sadler's Wells in the late 1970s. "I was perplexed but something sparked."[2] As he pursued his new interest, he was increasingly baffled by the elite image dance had acquired, given that it "had a certain freedom" in the way it could absorb contemporary trends and evolve.

By the time he came to Sadler's Wells, he was fully committed to democratisation. He wanted to run a theatre that would fling open its doors as wide as possible. Part of that was to make a commitment, in the spirit of Lilian Baylis, always to have 150 seats available for the lowest price possible – £12 in 2012. But the belief went further. "One of the things that has always motivated me is that I don't think theatres should just be for the white middle-classes. In my bones I want it to be a theatre for everyone. I know it can't be that because not everyone wants theatre and you are going to have to change the

Above: Franck II Louise at Breakin' Convention

whole world for that to happen. But I want to try my hardest to say, we want people to come."

In Jonzi D, he found the ideal collaborator. Born in Bow, in East London, the MC and poet had been involved in British hip hop culture, rapping and b-boying in clubs and on the streets, since its origins in the early 1980s. But he also took a CSE in dance and then studied contemporary dance at The Place. He used to go to Sadler's Wells before the theatre was rebuilt and remembers sitting in the old Upper Circle – "you had to go round the back to get in and it was dark" – to watch a performance by London Contemporary Dance. "It felt weird that everybody was completely silent." His instincts to do something different took him to the US to work with contemporary dance makers and then to devise his own form of "lyrical theatre" which combined rap with hip hop dance. As soon as he met Spalding they began to discuss the possibility of mounting a hip hop dance festival but Jonzi D was hesitant about putting on such an event at Sadler's Wells. "My doubts were less about it being here, more about it being done right, and when has anywhere like here done it right before?"

His vision was of a festival that was firmly based in an understanding of hip hop culture, of the way that it came from the streets and represented freedom of expression above all else. He wanted to liberate hip hop dance from its association with violence, misogyny, anger and death. He told the *Independent*: "The essence of hip hop culture has been obscured by bling bling monotony and designer gangsta rap. What happened to the skills? What happened to the originality? What happened to the unbridled creativity that shouted freedom? It's underground and it's alive."[3]

So when he started to organise the first Breakin' Convention, his aims were clear. He wanted to reveal hip hop as a thriving dance form, one whose originators were still alive and able to teach their skills to others. He also intended to give the growing British hip hop community, who had been showing their abilities in b-boy championships and battles in clubs, a chance to measure their talent against the opposition from Europe and the rest of the world, particularly Asia.

The first convention was the last legacy of Jean-Luc Choplin, who persuaded Bloomberg to sponsor the event in May 2004. With money behind him, Jonzi D was free to programme from the heart. On the first bill he brought in the Electric Boogaloos, West Coast founders of popping and boogaloo, who had not visited Britain in 25 years, and scheduled them alongside Tommy the Clown, progenitor of a new style called krumping, which at that time was hardly known in Britain except from Christina Aguilera's video for 'Dirty'.

Alongside these US pioneers, he programmed emerging British dance groups such as Boy Blue Entertainment and the Holloway Boyz, a crew from a north London school. He brought in Project Soul, the b-boy champions from South Korea, who dazzled with the way every single muscle seemed to move in perfect synchronicity, as they popped to plucked versions of Pachelbel and Mozart. There were workshops and master classes and there were also groups such as the Vagabond Crew from Paris, whose skills were harnessed by the choreographer Mohamed Berlabi into a longer piece of theatre that explored homelessness. "I am trying to look at the b-boy and the b-girl and see how they can create pieces of dance theatre," said Jonzi D. "How theatre can

Above: Freestyling in the Sadler's Wells foyer at Breakin' Convention

serve as a voice for us to articulate the entire experiences of the hip hop community."[4]

Despite some scepticism in advance, the reaction once the event was underway was overwhelmingly favourable, as people responded to the blast of fresh air hip hop brought in its wake. Clement Crisp was quick to understand the event's importance to the theatre. "That this particular celebration happened at Sadler's Wells is apt," he wrote. "Art for the people…was Miss Baylis's credo and from her endeavours sprang our National Theatre, the English National Opera and The Royal Ballet. Now her theatre hosts the newest dance made by the community. We must not betray her ideals."[5] Jonzi D acknowledged that it had all gone better than even he had imagined. "Sadler's Wells had said come in, we want you. It wasn't at all awkward. It was just electric."

His timing was perfect. Breakin' Convention hit its stride at the moment hip hop was emerging from the streets and making a charge into a far broader culture. By the time of the fifth event in 2009, hip hop dance shows by the German company Renegade, by a fledgling group called ZooNation and by Jonzi D himself had begun to enjoy a separate life at the Peacock Theatre, attracting enthusiastic crowds. That year, too, the dance group Diversity won *Britain's Got Talent*, a television talent show that at its peak was watched by 19 million people; in third place were another crew Flawless, who had themselves appeared at the 2008 convention.

Once street dance took centre stage on British television there was no stopping it, and hip hop became the most popular style exhibited on new shows such as the BBC's *So You Think You Can Dance* and Sky's *Got To Dance*. In the wake of Diversity's triumph, the London *Evening Standard* reported an increase of 850 a month

in the numbers of boys and men signing up for classes at Pineapple Studios. By 2010 Breakin' Convention was attracting record crowds, while the movie *Street Dance 3D,* which featured many of the British dancers who had performed at the convention, topped the British box office, grossing more in its opening weekend than any previous Lottery-funded effort.

But it wasn't just in terms of quantity that hip hop was making its mark. Standards were rising too. Being exposed to the world's finest dancers improved the works made by the British contingent, a feeling of feverish creativity underlined by the way in which old skool old-timers – the men who invented hip hop – were willing to pass on their knowledge to a new generation. On the pavement outside the theatre at the 2012 convention, passers-by were confronted with the sight of Lonnie "PopTart" Green, in a shiny zoot suit covered in flashing lights, instructing youngsters in the lost 1970s art of strutting.

Sadler's Wells was not alone in promoting hip hop dance. The Barbican played host to Boy Blue Entertainment, co-founded by Kenrick Sandy, one of the

Left: Jonzi D's *TAG...Me vs. The City*
Above: ZooNation Dance Company's *Some Like It Hip Hop*

choreographers of the Olympics opening ceremony and trail-blazers on the British scene; The Place, the Southbank Centre and many regional theatres gave their support. But from its inception Breakin' Convention provided a focus for many aspiring groups and choreographers. "It gives people the opportunity to get their crews together and showcase something," said Kate Prince. "It is a platform to start careers."

It also began to show new ways forward. Foreign companies such as the Brazilian Membros, who performed a shocking hour-long evocation of a brutalised society, or Compagnie Révolution from France, who made hypnotic works that combined ballet, hip-hop and contemporary dance, revealed the scope of hip hop as a dramatic art, one which had the potential to extend well beyond five-minute battles of pure technique. British choreographers took note.

Prince's own background, growing up in the New Forest, was far from typical. She was inspired to become a dancer and choreographer by MTV and particularly by the way Janet Jackson combined the influences of Broadway and hip hop. After teaching at Pineapple Studios, she formed her ZooNation Dance Company in 2002 and took their work to the Edinburgh Festival. By 2004, she was ready to make a leap of faith. She began to develop her ideas on a scheme run by The Place, but it was her mother who heard a piece on BBC Radio 4 about Breakin' Convention who suggested she should contact Sadler's Wells. "I wrote to Alistair and said you must programme us, and he did."

The first version of her breakthrough, *Into the Hoods*, emerged at the Peacock Theatre in a double bill with the work of Impact Dance, a more established dance company. It was smart and witty, with choreography that drew gasps from the audience and a story about Ruff Endz, a London council estate peopled by characters such as Spinderella, MC Rap-on-Zel and would-be loverboy Prince, that made them laugh. "It was the cheapest thing you have ever seen, but it had a full narrative and a sense of humour and I think they are the two things I always try to do," said Prince.

Picked up and developed by Phil McIntyre, a commercial producer, *Into the Hoods* opened at the Novello Theatre and became, in 2008, the first hip hop dance production in the West End. "It marked," said Luke Jennings in the *Observer*, "the evolution of British hip hop from a street form into a fully realised theatrical language."[6] He compared one gravity defying jump with a famously difficult butterfly leap in Ashton's *Les Patineurs*. This equivalence between the breathtaking brilliance of technique in ballet and hip hop – spinning on one leg as opposed to spinning on your head, if you like – was part of its early appeal for traditional dance audiences. But *Into the Hoods* went beyond technique and into a different realm: the vision Breakin' Convention had nurtured of a newly communicative art form had arrived.

The convention itself continues to reflect and encourage that shift in emphasis, casting its umbrella over a range of workshops and courses which enable young choreographers to develop distinctive work. At the 2012 convention, the results of such behind-the-scenes development were clear on stage in pieces such as *Broken Doll* in which Natalie James dramatically explored the issue of domestic violence or *Reverie* where Ivan Blackstock brought observational humour and Japanese theatre techniques to the creation of a nightmare with flying clothes.

Right: ZooNation Dance Company's *Into the Hoods* at the Novello Theatre

Over: Phase T at Breakin' Convention

The advantage of allowing British hip hop choreographers to find their own voice and forge a new style is clearest, however, in the growth of Kate Prince's work. In June 2010, she became an associate artist of Sadler's Wells and ZooNation became a resident company. Their next full-length piece, *Some Like It Hip Hop*, was premiered at the Peacock Theatre on November 1 2011 and showed just how far Prince had travelled in nine years.

This endearing and exhilarating inversion of the movie *Some Like It Hot* displayed all her old swagger and skill; indeed the energy of the finale, when wave after wave of thrilling virtuosic dancing swept the stage was more assured than anything she had created previously. But added to that was a new fluency and an absolute confidence in its story-telling. Prince and her collaborators Tommy Franzén and Carrie Anne Ingrouille used various styles of choreography to create and change the mood, creating romantic duets, agonised solos, and passages of both humour and power.

The show, which starred Tommy Franzén and Lizzie Gough, both familiar from *So You Think You Can Dance*, alongside Teneisha Bonner, was nominated for two Laurence Olivier awards and a South Bank Show award. It was pipped to the former by another Sadler's Wells production – Akram Khan's full-length solo *DESH*. Such success for a show developed at Sadler's Wells has benefits on all sides. "Sadler's Wells has been at the heart of encouraging us," Kate Prince said. "But it is a two-way relationship. We are bringing in an entirely new crowd of people."

It is not just commercially that the theatre has benefited; artistically too, the effect of hip hop has been invigorating. One of the most interesting premieres of

2012 was Russell Maliphant's *The Rodin Project*, which had a one-off performance as part of the biennal British Dance Edition. In this evocation of the work of the French sculptor Auguste Rodin, Maliphant cast three hip hop dancers – Franzén, Dickson Mbi and Ella Mesma – alongside his other dancers. Their presence gave a sculptural quality to the entire piece.

In the *Guardian* Judith Mackrell noted the way in which the section where the two men performed "a climbing duet on a high vertical plane, magically and fluidly adhering to its surface, suggests the life force pouring out of Rodin's masterpiece *The Gates of Hell*."[7] What Maliphant had seen at Breakin' Convention was the way in which hip hop can convey both weight and weightlessness. The muscular heft of the dancers gave them the rooted presence he sought – like Rodin's great carved hunks of stone and bronze – but the almost balletic way in which they could then float, burnished and altered the steps he was making.

As time goes on, increasing numbers of choreographers will make similar discoveries and hip hop dance will not only continue to develop in its own way, but will also enhance other dance forms. When the full history of 21st-century dance is written, hip hop will be a huge part of the story and Breakin' Convention makes Sadler's Wells central to that tale. As Michael Hulls, lighting designer on *The Rodin Project* said: "I think the fact that a major dance house with the history and reputation of Sadler's Wells recognised that this was something that had potential to develop as a language, as an art form, changed the way that people thought about it."

Right: Russell Maliphant's *The Rodin Project*

8

CHRISTOPHER WHEELDON AND THE BALLETIC TRADITION

The history of Sadler's Wells is not just engrained in its spirit. It is stamped on the fabric of the building too, most notably in the glass-covered glimpse of the old well that greets the audience on its way into the stalls. There is a Lilian Baylis studio theatre where performances happen, and Ashton, Lesley Edwards and Gillian Lynne studios where works are made. Visitors can host their receptions in The Fonteyn Room. There is no physical space named after Ninette de Valois, but her portrait in oils gazes sternly out across the corridor as you walk to the stage door; another, rather more inspiring, photograph of her teaching students in the old school hangs in Alistair Spalding's office upstairs.

Despite British ballet's enormous debt to de Valois, it is difficult to guess what she would have made of the modern scene. While she would have applauded her old theatre's consistent desire to inspire and promote the best new work, some of the results might have prompted her disapproval. "Contemporary Dance in its early years of structure – the days of undiluted Martha Graham schooling – had something of much value to give us," she wrote firmly. "Unfortunately Contemporary Dance today seems to think in reverse. They seem to have decided that we have much more to give to them! We are showing the same tendency and are not helped by finding ourselves all stuck under the same umbrella with an ambiguous title of 'Dance'. I naturally hope that all the above is a foolish phase. Purity and integrity of approach is needed on all sides."[1]

Those words which appeared in Kathrine Sorley Walker's 1987 biography could barely be uttered in today's landscape, where contemporary dance and classical ballet cross-fertilise each other to such an extent that Wayne McGregor is the resident choreographer of

The Royal Ballet and a Royal Ballet-trained dancer such as Russell Maliphant incorporates elements of ballet, capoeira and hip hop into his own distinctive works. Even Christopher Wheeldon talked in interviews of wanting to make classical and contemporary dance "hold hands".[2]

Yet of all the Sadler's Wells associate artists it is Wheeldon who has the most direct link with the de Valois lineage. Born in Yeovil, he was inspired to dance by watching, on television, Frederick Ashton's *La Fille mal gardée*, that defining statement of the English style. He trained at The Royal Ballet School and remembered performing at the decrepit Sadler's Wells in a schools performance when he was a junior associate. "Backstage it was all leaky, hissing pipes and it felt a bit wartime and historical, but also grotty." But in 1993, at the age of 19 he left the Royal, put himself on a flight to New York and talked himself into the New York City Ballet. By 1997 he had become that company's resident choreographer.

From that moment, Wheeldon was regarded as the great lost hope of British neo-classical choreography, someone who should never have been allowed to leave the country. As he developed a style which combined the clean, classical line and fleet, lyrical movements that he had acquired in his Royal Ballet training with the dynamism, attack and strength that he had encountered in New York, he became one of the leading choreographers in the world. He was routinely described as the man carrying the torch for a particular school of balletic pointe shoe choreography into the 21st century. Only Alexei Ratmansky, former director of the Bolshoi, kept him company in this lonely mission. Like Ratmansky, Wheeldon made both his affiliation to ballet and his determination to preserve it as an art form crystal clear.

"I would just like it not to be dead in 20 years time. It feels like it is really teetering."[3]

In his time at New York City Ballet, Wheeldon built up an extensive freelance career, choreographing works for the Royal, San Francisco and Bolshoi Ballets among others. His defining style was abstract; his musicality seemed to make the steps part of the score, but he also, unusually, managed to suggest both hidden narrative and emotion. People loved his exceptional fluency and inventiveness. So when, in 2007, he announced that he was setting up his own transatlantic company called Morphoses, that would divide its time between Sadler's Wells and New York's City Centre, the level of expectation was spectacular. "It is the scale of his ambitions that will delight those with a passion for ballet," said Mark Brown in the *Guardian*. "Wheeldon admits that he is setting the bar extremely high, taking inspiration from Sergei Diaghilev." It was left to Wheeldon himself to inject a note of caution: "You see new companies coming and going all the time and this is a huge gamble."[4]

Alistair Spalding was one of the first people to whom Wheeldon had confided his plans. They had come to know each other when Benjamin Millepied (later famous as the choreographer of *Black Swan* and the husband of Natalie Portman) brought a company of NYCB soloists to Sadler's Wells under the title Danses Concertantes in 2004; one of the works they performed was Wheeldon's *Polyphonia*. When he heard Wheeldon's plans for Morphoses, Spalding was both immediately supportive and excited about the idea of having a contemporary ballet company linked to Sadler's Wells. He agreed that the theatre would provide technical support, rehearsal space and commission a new work each season. When *The Times* suggested that the idea was both "extraordinarily

Left: Christopher Wheeldon's *Fool's Paradise*
Over: Christopher Wheeldon's *Commedia*

ambitious and seriously expensive", Spalding was confident. "We have found lots of people willing to support this venture because there is so much excitement around it. Christopher is a great choreographer who is looking for collaborations to make something different happen with ballet and he is definitely a draw for private sponsorship."[5]

If Wheeldon felt the pressure, he did not show it. His default mode was calm good humour as he patiently explained his aims. He wanted to encourage collaborations between artists from different disciplines and to bring in the best artists, designers, photographers and composers to work with his company. His goal was to have a permanent roster of dancers by 2009, but in its initial stages the company would be a scratch troupe of guest artists, some of them very starry indeed. The first performances would see Wendy Whelan and Craig Hall of the New York City Ballet, as well as Johan Kobborg

Above: Christopher Wheeldon's *After The Rain*

and Alina Cojocaru of The Royal Ballet in works he had choreographed. Economics played a part in these early decisions: because he would not have to pay himself royalties, it was easier to load the programmes with his own pieces than with more expensive ones by other choreographers. Yet it was also his work as well as his vision that audiences wanted to see.

He made two new pieces for the company's first visit to Sadler's Wells in September 2007. The first was a delicate pas de deux for Kobborg and Cojocaru to the andante from Prokofiev's violin concerto. The second was a considerably more ambitious piece to a score by Joby Talbot, originally called *The Dying Swan*, and designed as the soundtrack to a silent film. Wheeldon wanted to try to work with Talbot since he was already thinking about him as the possible composer of a new full-length ballet he had been commissioned to stage at Covent Garden. (An idea that turned, in 2011, into *Alice's Adventures in Wonderland*.) For their first collaboration, he asked him to turn his piano score into one for the full orchestra which Sadler's Wells had suggested he used.

Then, over a period of weeks at the Vail International Festival, in New York and in the rehearsal rooms at Sadler's Wells, he set to work on the choreography. His habitual method is to get to know the music inside out, and to walk into the studio "fairly empty". "The music is already playing in my body in a sense. But then, more often than not, it's a case of let's see what we can create together." In the case of *Fool's Paradise*, he wanted to make an abstract work that captured the essence of a silent film. "Abstract ballets can quite often feel lost in a void of diffuse movement; they need a real sense of time and place."

With its nine dancers clad in nude tunics and tights, and lit with a golden glow, *Fool's Paradise* had a dreamlike quality, revealing Wheeldon's ability to shape lyrical dance that moved between sharply defined, sculpted tableaux for groups of dancers and a swooning, lush romanticism as they broke into pairs and trios. Wendy Whelan and Craig Hall were particularly mesmerising. "As the two of them dance – he coolly noble, she unrolling in his arms like a bale of silk – flakes of gold leaf drift down from the flies. This sounds very Celine Dion, I know, but it was actually rather wonderful,"[6] wrote Luke Jennings.

The problem was that *Fool's Paradise* was not performed on the opening night; a mistake, as Wheeldon acknowledged in retrospect. Instead an over-excited audience were served with a revival of his 2002 work actually called *Morphoses*, sleek but restrained in tone, and then three pas de deux – the Prokofiev, one by Edwaard Liang, and *Slingerland* by William Forsythe. All had their merits but none made much impact. In my review I said, "The evening is so prim and buttoned up, it turns what was a white-hot ticket into a very lukewarm attraction. You long for someone to rip off their clothes and run on screaming."[7] That was more or less what happened next, when in Wheeldon's *After the Rain*, made for NYCB in 2005 to music by Arvo Pärt, Wendy Whelan and Craig Hall performed a duet of such blistering emotion and tender loveliness that it lit up the theatre. Though the audience rose to its feet in rapture, many critics were downbeat. The reception of the second bill, which featured *Fool's Paradise*, was considerably warmer.

Although Wheeldon later admitted that he felt he could have been cut a little slack, he took notice of what was said and was willing to learn. In this endeavour, he was helped by the attitude of Sadler's Wells. "I was never made to feel any pressure about whether the house was sold out. Alistair would say, 'We know we are taking a risk. Don't worry about it, just create', which is great for an artist to hear."

In fact, the 2008 visit of Morphoses (which was also receiving support from the City Centre in New York) was well received. Its line-up kept Whelan, but also included a new discovery, 15-year-old Beatrix Stix-Brunell, and The Royal Ballet duo Edward Watson and Leanne Benjamin. Wheeldon introduced the bill from the stage, believing that by explaining dance he could make it more accessible to new audiences. "The more we give away, the more we'll draw people in".[8] In this case, he suggested that the evening would follow Stravinsky's dictum of looking to the past to be inspired by the future. To this end, he programmed Frederick Ashton's *Monotones II*, Jerome Robbins' *Other Dances*, alongside his own *Polyphonia*, made in 2001, and a fine statement of his musicality and inventiveness.

Wheeldon's new work was *Commedia*, an attempt to make sense of Stravinsky's *Pulcinella* score, commissioned by Diaghilev. A gentle tribute to *commedia dell' arte* with period costumes that were discarded to reveal the dancers tights and leotards, it was full of gentle humour and clever touches. Its highlights were a playful duet for Watson and Benjamin, defined by cheeky pats and insouciant gestures, and a spiky one for Benjamin and Stix-Brunell which seemed to play on their respective ages. A second programme repeated *Commedia* and *Fool's Paradise* and introduced a new work by the choreographer Emily Molnar. The company seemed full of energy and promise.

By 2009, however, some of that vigour was draining away. Wheeldon had always promised that he would be running a permanent company by this time; but he had

launched Morphoses just as the world economy started to tilt into recession. He never raised enough money either to set up a proper administration or employ his chosen dancers all year round, though he was still putting a brave face on it. "We're a bit like the Obama campaign. We raised $59,000 in $10 and $20 bills."[9] For the first time, the programming showed the strain. Wheeldon could only afford one bill with an orchestra and gave that opportunity to the Australian choreographer Tim Harbour who produced *Leaving Songs*, which was not to the taste of any critic; Lightfoot and Leon's *Softly As I Leave You* was innocuous but vacuous and though the revival of *Commedia* was once more a delight, the hit of the evening was Alexei Ratmansky's energetically witty take on Ravel's *Bolero*.

For the second programme, accompanied only by piano, Wheeldon revived his fine *Continuum*. It featured what Ismene Brown called "the Whelan moment"[10], a pas de deux that cast into shadow everything that had gone before. This astounding ballerina always brought out the best in Wheeldon and she also illuminated *Rhapsody Fantaisie*, his new piece, to Rachmaninov, yet its overall effect was muted. "By his own standards, this new piece is a slight disappointment," I wrote at the time. "It often feels grounded when you expect it to fly."[11]

In fact, the need to fundraise and the inability to keep hold of a permanent company were sapping Wheeldon's desire to go on with his bold experiment. By the end of 2009, Morphoses had reached only about a fifth of its targeted budget, and was lurching from one short season to the next. In 2010, Wheeldon announced that he was leaving his own company. They had danced 30 ballets, eight of which were new, but they had never achieved their aim of making work that would reach out to new

Right: Christopher Wheeldon's *Rhapsody Fantasie*

Left: Emily Molnar's *Six Fold Illuminate*, performed by Morphoses

audiences, and wished-for collaborations with artists such as Björk had failed to come off.

The struggle that Wheeldon found in raising cash in the US, where sponsorship and giving tends to be concentrated round the gilt-edged galas and established art forms, throws Sadler's Wells' success in continuing to back creative gambles into sharp relief. "They are prepared to be in the position of losing money in order to create interesting new work," he explained.

Sadler's Wells was faced with the same recession as the rest of the theatre world, but instead of limiting its ambitions, it cut back on the extras, while leaving the artistic programme intact. The expensive Spring Dance at the Coliseum which brought companies such as New York City Ballet to London faltered, but Sadler's Wells' own programme did not thanks, in part, to a pattern of scheduling whereby the less obviously popular projects initially run for a few days while shows that are likely to draw huge crowds are allowed longer on stage. Morphoses, for example, used to perform for a maximum of five days, concentrating its audience and keeping costs down. When William Forsythe wanted to close the upper circle because he felt the audience was too far away, he was allowed to do so, but the performances ran for two rather than three nights.

Works that are broad in appeal make the theatre money, which in turn is ploughed back into adventurous commissioning. Yet this economic necessity to welcome as many people as possible, has also yielded an artistic bonus. "It makes Sadler's Wells a theatre for the people, it isn't just a highbrow place," Wheeldon observed. "It's only the dance aficionados who are going to see quite a lot of the new work, but the more popular shows make it somewhere everyone wants to go." In this sense, the

theatre has become an ambassador for the arts as a whole, a place that makes a virtue of the circumstances in which it has to operate.

Morphoses was also a boon. It created excitement about the possibilities of ballet as a contemporary form and in so doing, reminded people that Sadler's Wells was the place to go to see all dance, ballet included. In 2007, after seeing their autumn season in New York, Spalding booked American Ballet Theatre into Sadler's Wells, even though they are a famously expensive company to import. To defray costs, he charged £70 for the top price ticket, convinced that there was an audience that would pay to see a world-famous company that had not visited London for 17 years. The same logic applied when the Mariinsky Ballet came to the theatre in 2008, revealing their classical supremacy in two programmes, one a tribute to William Forsythe and one, conducted by Valery Gergiev which made Balanchine's *Apollo* and *The Prodigal Son* look fresh minted. ABT returned the

following year. Audiences came, admired and paid the ticket prices, though the £12 rock-bottom tickets were also preserved.

After the closure of Morphoses, Wheeldon returned to his freelance career. "It was a brilliant experiment, but I did what I had to do. I had to draw a line".[12] In 2012, when Kevin O'Hare took over the artistic directorship of The Royal Ballet, he invited Wheeldon, whose action-packed *Alice* had been one of the great hits of the previous year, to become an associate choreographer. The appointment means that the two dance houses of London are now closer than they have ever been; they share not only two associates, but also similar ambitions to energise ballet and make it more appealing to a younger audience. Wheeldon, with all he learnt from Morphoses, will be at the centre of that pursuit. In a turn of events of which Dame Ninette might very well have approved, *Fool's Paradise* was announced as one of the works in The Royal Ballet's 2012 season.

Above: Christopher Wheeldon's *Continuum*

9

IN THE SPIRIT OF DIAGHILEV

AND HOW TO COMMISSION NEW WORK

2009 marked the centenary of the founding of the Ballets Russes, one of the most significant moments in 20th-century art. It was an anniversary that prompted a great deal of musing about how it was that Sergei Diaghilev, an ambitious and talented young impresario, had managed to create a dance company that changed the world. He did so almost by accident since he intended to bring a season of Russian opera to the West in 1909 and only changed tack when one of his wealthiest backers pulled out. Thanks to the fact that ballet was cheaper, he switched art form and an influential legend was born.

His company featured dancers of almost mythological importance such as Vaslav Nijinsky and Tamara Karsavina. But it also nurtured choreographers who transformed the nature of dance and laid the foundations of the modern repertoire: Fokine, Nijinsky, Nijinska, Massine, Balanchine. In Marie Rambert and Ninette de Valois, it employed and inspired the two women who built British ballet. As if that was not enough, it set an example of collaborative inspiration that every company since has sought to follow, by persuading the best artists and composers to place their gifts at the service of ballet. Stravinsky, Debussy, Satie and Ravel were all commissioned by Diaghilev; so were the designers Benois, Bakst and Redon, not to mention Picasso and Matisse. By pushing ballet to the forefront of avant-garde culture, Diaghilev made it more significant than it had ever been before.

It is one thing to recognise that Diaghilev's achievement was extraordinary, quite another to know how to celebrate it, particularly since part of the importance of Ballets Russes was its shocking novelty, a quality inevitably lost in historical reconstruction. Some of Diaghilev's ballets – *The Firebird*, *Les Noces* and *Apollo*, for example – still look

Left: Sidi Larbi Cherkaoui's *Faun*

like masterpieces. But when works such as *Schéhérazade* and *Le Spectre de la rose* are dusted off, they can feel like period pieces. Nijinsky's *L'Après-midi d'un faune* once caused a scandal with its explicit sexuality; now it looks quaint. In the case of *Le Sacre du printemps*, which famously caused a riot in 1913, the power of Stravinsky's monumental music remains, but Nijinsky's steps are lost. In recreation, they appear odd rather than radical.

Given such difficulties, Sadler's Wells decided to celebrate Ballets Russes not through the works themselves, but by concentrating on the courage and vision behind them. Diaghilev's starting point for the 20-year blaze of brilliance that his company represented was to ask whether it "would be possible to create a number of short, new ballets, which, besides being of artistic value, would link the three main factors, music, decorative design and choreography far more".[1] It was that collaborative attitude that Sadler's Wells would try to replicate. Spalding commissioned four choreographers to work with leading designers and musicians on four entirely new pieces for an evening called *In the Spirit of Diaghilev*. Debra Craine understood the point. "Four world premieres on a single night? No one could accuse Alistair Spalding…of thinking small. But then neither did Sergei Diaghilev."[2]

Each of the choreographers – Wayne McGregor, Russell Maliphant, Sidi Larbi Cherkaoui and Javier De Frutos – approached the commission from a different standpoint. For *Dyad 1909*, McGregor took a characteristically sidelong look at the project. Noting that the polar explorer Ernest Shackleton found the magnetic South Pole in the year that Ballets Russes was founded – and that a plane flew over it 20 years later, when Diaghilev died – he decided to make an Antarctic-flavoured piece

marking that period of scientific endeavour. He was working with a new score from the Icelandic composer Olafur Arnalds, and designs by the artists Jane and Louise Wilson, who are twin sisters. Cognitive scientists from California were recruited to help him examine the nature of collaboration itself, watching the piece as it was created.

For Russell Maliphant, after the complexities of scale and collaboration required by *Eonnagata* the appeal of *AfterLight (Part One)* was that, "I was dying to do something simple, just with movement and light and one dancer." Enlisting the help of the animator Jan Urbanowski gave Michael Hulls a chance to work with projected light. *Faun*, the contribution of Sidi Larbi Cherkaoui, at Spalding's suggestion, used the original Debussy music, but the choreographer chose to disrupt it with a new score from Nitin Sawhney. The resulting duet, which had costumes by the fashion designer Hussein Chalayan, was inspired by Nijinsky's bravery. "As an artist he had an absolute vision of what he wanted to create and then he faced the results from the audience. It must have really hurt him,"[3] Cherkaoui said.

Those words proved eerily prophetic when it came to the final commission from Javier De Frutos. Well-known as a provocateur, and famous in his youth for dancing nude, De Frutos set out to create a scandal. Taking Jean Cocteau as his starting point, and the music of Ravel's La Valse – rejected by Diaghilev as "not suitable for ballet" – he created a piece called *Eternal Damnation to Sancho and Sanchez*. "Nothing you can do today would be scandalous anymore except for annoying the Catholic Church. So that is my target."[4]

Spalding failed to see the storm clouds coming. "When we saw the run-through we didn't think it would cause the controversy that it did." But perhaps no one could have predicted the scenes when the work was premiered on October 14 2009. "Even Diaghilev might have been shocked," said Judith Mackrell, noting that the audience had witnessed "some of the most graphic scenes of sex and violence seen on the dance stage."[5]

In front of Katrina Lindsey's priapic pink designs and underneath a neon sign saying "Amuse me!" – one translation of Diaghilev's words to Cocteau – De Frutos had set a horror story with a hunchbacked Pope, pregnant nuns and horny priests, mouthing obscenities and performing grotesque acts. The choreography was eloquent, but the piece was vulgar and deliberately offensive. People stormed out, and at the conclusion – where the Pope was electrocuted, shortly after one of the nuns had been garrotted with her own rosary – loud boos filled the auditorium. Clement Crisp was furious, accusing *Eternal Damnation* of "an insolence that disgraced the evening." "That it was staged at all seems to me inexplicable,"[6] he fumed.

In retrospect, Spalding believed that part of the problem was one of expectation; people did not imagine they would witness something so shocking at the conclusion of what was effectively a tribute evening. He felt, however, that the controversy was totally in the spirit of Diaghilev. But the reaction had repercussions. Despite having wished to goad attitudes, the vehemence of the response took De Frutos aback. The BBC pulled out of broadcasting his segment of the bill in a pre-watershed slot on BBC4 and he received death threats which, he said, "affected my health greatly". "I got scared of anything and everybody,"[7] he told the *Independent*. Spalding went on the offensive, writing in the *Guardian* that while he did not want to attack the BBC, he was glad that "as an artistic director working in live theatre I can still, with appropriate warnings, show work which hovers on the edge of what is acceptable to audiences."

"There is no such thing as great art that is safe and appeals to all," he argued. "I believe that part of the furore over Javier's work and its ability to shock is that no one realised that a piece of choreography could do this. Most take the view that dance is a rather effete art form that deals only with truth and beauty. The reality is that dance is often disturbing, ugly, confrontational, violent and sometimes sexually explicit."[8] Liz Hoggard, writing in the *Standard* agreed. "The shock of the new isn't supposed to be easy," she said. "It is your duty to go along and be annoyed."[9] What the row proved categorically, and rather gratifyingly for those who cared about its future, was that dance could still ruffle feathers. It wasn't all pretty girls in tutus, it was, as in Diaghilev's time, worthy of its place at the centre of the cultural debate.

Above: Russell Maliphant's *AfterLight (Part One)*
Right: Wayne McGregor's *Dyad 1909*

With its in-your-face shock tactics, De Frutos' *Damnation* was also an extreme example of Spalding's belief that part of the function of Sadler's Wells as a commissioning house had to be its willingness to allow creators to experiment – and sometimes to fail. "There will always be those pieces that aren't quite as successful as others but if they are done with the right intention and integrity then you will learn as much from them. You have to have faith that everything is going to work but then you have to have the possibility of putting it into perspective when it doesn't and to be mature about that."

In the Spirit of Diaghilev represented exactly the creative freedom that Sadler's Wells had been trying to encourage in that it gave all its participants a chance for self-discovery. In the case of Russell Maliphant, it laid the foundation for another astonishing work. His *AfterLight (Part One)* was inspired by photographs of Nijinsky, by the extreme plasticity of his rounded arms, the way his body seemed to fall in to sculptural shapes, and by the spirals that he drew as he descended, at the height of his success with Ballets Russes, into schizophrenia and madness. But it was also informed by the interest in the working of light on stage that Maliphant and Hulls had explored throughout their careers.

In September 2007, in another Sadler's Wells commission, they had worked with the artist Isaac Julien on a piece called *Cast No Shadow*, and had noticed the potential of projected light on dancers. It was during that collaboration, too, that Maliphant met Daniel Proietto, a charismatic dancer perfectly suited to his work. In *AfterLight (Part One)*, it was Proietto he set spinning and torquing in a circle of

expanding and contracting dappled light. The effect was a pitch-perfect and profoundly moving evocation of Nijinsky's lost sanity.

This was a work that would never have come into being without the initial commission from Sadler's Wells. "You usually wouldn't have the freedom to make a 15-minute piece; to get project funding you have got to make a full evening's work," Maliphant explained. That first solo prompted him to continue to explore the idea of Nijinsky and led to a full-length work which was premiered at Sadler's Wells in 2010. Eventually, in another radical step, it would tour along with Wayne McGregor's *UNDANCE* and Cherkaoui's *Faun*, under the collective title *Made at Sadler's Wells*, making a full evening of dance that sprang from the way in which Sadler's Wells had exerted its power as a producer and generator of new work.

UNDANCE, too, had its distant origins in the *In the Spirit of Diaghilev* night – though the seed that was planted was from an experiment that did not entirely succeed. As another associate artist Akram Khan had noted in a different context, "the pieces you should hold closest to are the ones you fail with." He was talking

about the way that works can be developed with the best intentions and hold great potential, but then go wrong. If you can recognise why that happens, he argued, it helps you to grow as an artist. It is something Wayne McGregor also believes. "What is a bad piece? Is it bad for the artist, or is it bad for the person watching? A bad piece can actually be the most important piece you make." Encountering problems and finding ways to surmount them, "is a way to extend your choreographic palate and I think this is the future of creativity."

In making *Dyad 1909*, a work that was warmly if not ecstatically received, he discovered that the challenge of working with the Wilson twins was that they rarely agreed with each other. "They are brilliant and that is interesting for their work when there's just the two of them, but it's quite hard when you're working with five people." The result was that they presented him with a set containing multiple projections, when he expected only one. In a discussion of this, before the premiere, he quoted Merce Cunningham: "When you go out into the countryside and you see a tree, you walk around it. You don't wish it wasn't there." He said that he relished the demands presented by the

Above: Russell Maliphant's *AfterLight (Part One)*
Right and over: Wayne McGregor, Mark-Anthony Turnage and Mark Wallinger's *UNDANCE*

unexpected. "It is really interesting to work with people you don't know, because it is only by mixing the ecology of the way you think with other people who think differently that you start to evolve."[10]

In McGregor's case, the experience of working with film precipitated an interest in its effects on stage. This led first to *Live Fire Exercise*, for The Royal Ballet, which unfolded in front of digitalised images of a desert laid waste by military action. But it also prompted ideas that found their way into *UNDANCE*, a bold collaboration with the composer Mark-Anthony Turnage and the artist Mark Wallinger.

McGregor had been talking to Wallinger about making a piece together ever since they met at a South Bank Show awards in 2001, but it was Spalding, who wanted to commission a new score from Turnage, who added the composer to the equation. In doing so, he was moving onto new ground, throwing his own ideas into the mix. "This is more artistic producing than simply supporting work that artists want to make," McGregor noted.

What was unusual about the *UNDANCE* triumvirate was that they were all artists of equal star-power, pre-eminent in their different fields. Different too, was the

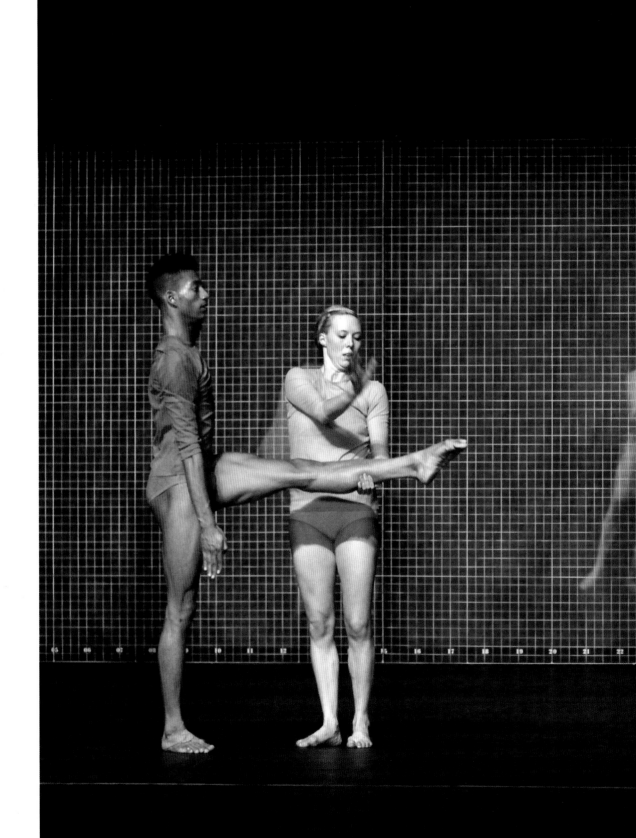

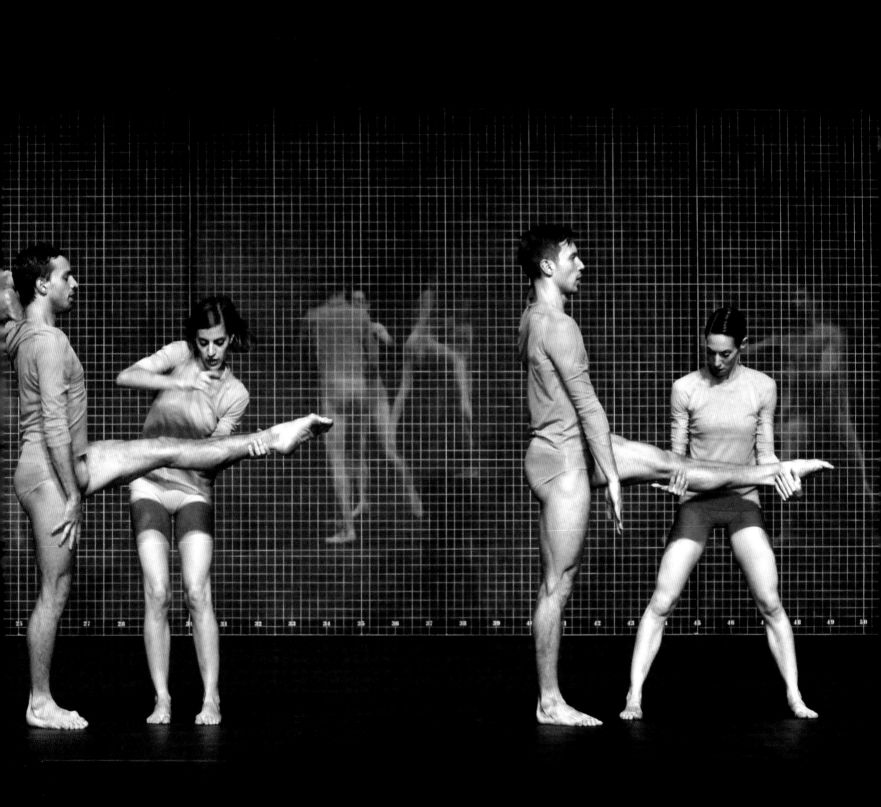

way Wallinger took the lead. "I thought if I am going to have any meaningful role in this process, I am going to have to be the instigator in some sense," he said.[11] He presented the group with a little book, like a conceptual artwork in miniature, in which he outlined a group of interwoven thoughts. He talked about the work of the photographic pioneer Eadweard Muybridge, who pinioned human movement within a grid of measurement, and then linked this with Alberti's window, which Renaissance painters used to establish perspective. Alongside Muybridge's list of the verbs he photographed and animated, he placed the list of actions compiled by the sculptor Richard Serra. For good measure, he threw in Newton's laws of motion, Michael Jackson's moonwalk and the idea of the UN un-doing the problems caused by war and unrest.

For McGregor to be presented with so complex an idea at so early a stage was another new way of working. But, however unsettling, such intense collaboration was exactly what he had hoped for. Turnage meanwhile went away and produced his own, entirely separate response to Wallinger's propositions. When the three strands of thought came together on stage in December 2011, it was obvious that a certain alchemy had been at work. The dancers of Random, in flesh-coloured costumes which recalled Muybridge's nude figures enacted a series of action verbs: skipping, throwing, and jumping. Behind them, on a replica of the grid, a film of the same dancers played slightly out of synch; at one point running in the opposite direction to their steps on stage, making them appear to push through time itself. Turnage's stirring score, in eight movements, added to the rich brew. It was stringent yet stunning.

This airily beautiful yet deeply thoughtful piece sprung not only from Spalding's policy of creative commissions, but also from all that had gone before it, not least the films in *Dyad 1909*. If you look back over the history of dance, this is often how it works. When people talk of Diaghilev commissioning Picasso, it is easy to forget that one of the results was *Parade* – a silly Cubist sensation, quickly forgotten. When we talk of Balanchine's *Apollo*, one of the pieces that still dazzles, it is important to remember that in the same 1928 season the Ballets Russes premiered, with equally high hopes, Massine's *Ode*, which was a flop.

In the same way, when de Valois laid the foundations for the British repertory, the enduring successes of the Vic-Wells Ballet such as Ashton's *Les Rendezvous* and her own *The Rake's Progress* took their place alongside ill-received works such as his *Cupid and Psyche*, made in 1939 and booed by the gallery, and her *Orpheus and Eurydice*. Indeed she actively advocated deliberately dropping a couple of works at the end of each season to clear the way for novelty.

Yet dance makers in modern times are under enormous pressure only to make works that will replicate the success they have had before. Bogged down in funding applications, worried about finding audiences and filling theatres, they can end up frightened to take risks. In promoting a spirit of adventure, advocating imaginative match-making between different disciplines, and finding enough money and resilience to ride the disappointing results as well as the successes, Sadler's Wells is making a great contribution to dance in the early 21st century.

As Luke Jennings once remarked: "If anyone can lay claim to the fur-collared overcoat of Sergei Diaghilev, it is probably Alistair Spalding."[12]

10

HOFESH SHECHTER
AND THE FUTURE

Above: Hofesh Shechter's *In Your Rooms*

Out of a pitch black stage, a voice emerges. "If you think of the cosmos, it's a complex thing." Cue ferocious drum beats and a quick-fire sequence of scenes in which, in alternating flashes of darkness and light, crouched figures engaged in repetitive, rocking movements are juxtaposed with a single man whirring his arm like a demented banshee or a couple grappling with each other. Suddenly darkness descends once more and the voice says: "I can do much better than that." Silence. "No, I can't" – and the sequence begins again.

This was the thrilling opening of Hofesh Shechter's *In Your Rooms*, one of the most visceral, explosive works ever seen on the Sadler's Wells stage, a piece which clearly signposted the way to the future. Gerald Dowler, writing in the *Financial Times*, caught the mood of a shell-shocked and exhilarated audience. "How often do you see something of the moment, at the edge of hipness, which also has substance, is obviously the product of a serious creative process and stays with you beyond the performance?"[1]

Shechter was always special. He arrived at Sadler's Wells courtesy of a device known as "the London escalator", a mode of transport built to propel him from obscurity to fame, from a tiny stage to a large one. The journey began when John Ashford, visionary director of The Place spotted Shechter's potential, and brokered a deal with the Arts Council and his friend Alistair Spalding at Sadler's Wells as well as Julia Carruthers, dance producer at the South Bank Centre, whereby the 32-year-old choreographer would make a piece that would move within six months from The Place (300 seats), through the Queen Elizabeth Hall (900 seats) to Sadler's Wells (1,500 seats), growing as it went.

Shechter's reaction to the idea was joy, followed swiftly by pure panic. "Sadler's was like the Mecca of contemporary dance." But though the commission was an act of faith on the part of all his backers, it was based on clear and convincing indications of an idiosyncratic and important talent.

Born in Israel, Shechter had danced with the Batsheva Dance Company but came first to Paris and then to London in 2002 because he wanted "to be alive". His initial plan had been to pursue a career as a drummer, but he quickly ran out of money and returned to dancing, with his compatriot Jasmin Vardimon's company, in order to earn his living. After 18 months, however, the urge to make his own work was too strong to resist and in 2004 his piece *Cult* won the audience prize in the annual choreography competition known as The Place Prize. That was when Ashford spotted his potential: two years later *Uprising*, a sharply observed all-male piece about men and their behaviour, revealed that talent fully formed.

With its powerful pulse and filmic lighting *Uprising* showed Shechter's most distinctive quality as a choreographer: his works are full of existential darkness and doubt, but the excitement of the steps means that their effect is uplifting rather than angst-ridden. They engulf you with their insistent vision, making it impossible not to feel exhilarated by them.

This originality springs partly from the way that he writes his own music, percussive sounds played at ear-splitting volume so that the intensity of the sound becomes part of the dance itself. But the choreography also marches to a different drum. It may draw on many influences from William Forsythe to the folk dance tradition in which Shechter first trained, from contemporary technique to hip hop, but they are all melded into swooping, flexible patterns which seem furious and fluid at one and the same moment.

The starting point for *In Your Rooms* was Shechter's feeling "of trying to be invisible and not make too much noise". He wanted to follow "a lost individual in the pathetically organised world we have created". But its absolute foundation was a 20-second snatch of viola playing, which he listened to on a loop for about a month, letting it seep into his consciousness. That tiny fragment became the root of the entire score; this is the way he always works, making little sketches of sound, searching for exactly the right snippet to define the atmosphere of the piece. "It is a bit like catching a butterfly."

Moving *In Your Rooms* through three theatres in such a short space of time gave Shechter an opportunity to return repeatedly to the studio and develop his ideas. Such perspective is very rare. "It is always difficult just to say OK we will have four weeks back in the studio," he said. But you could see the results on stage. At each venue, the piece improved and deepened. By the time it reached Sadler's Wells on September 27 2007 it was ready to be a sensation.

The evening in fact opened with *Uprising*, seven men striding towards the audience in swirling smoke and dazzling spotlights. "Instantly, you're hooked," said Mark Monahan in the *Daily Telegraph*.[2] But this was as nothing compared to the impact of *In Your Rooms*. With his dancers forming a frieze, and the musicians glimpsed above their heads, Shechter wove an immense tapestry of sound and motion: at one moment the entire company, dressed in clothes that look as if they have just walked in from the street, seemed to batter the sky with their fists. At another they whirred around on one leg while shaking the other like demented folk dancers. They made tiny ritualistic gestures with their hands while shifting their

weight from one side to the other, falling into the floor and rising from it without any apparent effort.

The lighting carved the stage into segments so figures emerged as if by magic. Sometimes the spotlights picked out individual dancers, convulsed in what looked like grief or fear; at other moments, massed ranks of shapes squirmed in the darkness. The motion unfolded in a constant flow; everything was seamless, synchronised, and compelling. The piece was full of doubt and pain, yet as Debra Craine noted in *The Times*, "the contrast between the bleakness of the work's emotional territory and the sheer thrill of its realisation is striking."[3]

Shechter compared the effect of the premiere to one of those 1930s movies where newspaper headlines spin towards the camera in rapid motion. "It was really ridiculous from the day after the last show." The exposure provided by a debut on the Sadler's Wells stage had made his talent noticed all over the world. "It took me six months to understand what was going on and to enjoy it and do my best with it." By the end of 2008, he had formed his own permanent company, won the Dance Critics' Circle award for best modern choreography, reinforced his cool credentials by choreographing the title sequence for the TV drama series *Skins*, and become an associate artist at Sadler's Wells. By early in 2009, he had been commissioned by the theatre to take "the choreographer's cut" of *In Your Rooms* – with 21 musicians and 17 dancers – to the Roundhouse, where it achieved the status of a rock concert not a dance event.

It was heady stuff, but Shechter's nerve held. "Expectation is always there and you can either take it as a negative pressure or a positive pressure that cooks something. It can be something that helps you trust yourself and experiment more because you realise people

are willing to come on this journey." In this, he was helped not only by the solid support of Sadler's Wells, but also by the Brighton Dome which offered his company a berth and was the setting for his next work, *The Art of Not Looking Back*, an all-female piece for six women to balance the testosterone-fuelled *Uprising*. But much was still riding on *Political Mother*, his first full-length piece due to be unveiled at the Brighton Festival in May 2010 before transferring to Sadler's Wells.

The idea came to him sitting on the top of a bus, going home from Islington, and wondering what to make his next work about. It struck him that London was full of parallel realities, where people could live in streets next to each other but have entirely different experiences. "We know that horrible things are happening but we are able to create a bubble of survival that keeps us sane." He began to write down seven or eight different images, which he envisaged unfolding on stage like scattered scenes in a film. Music was once again integral to the concept. He found what he described as "a thundering groove which feels as if it is riding forward over time" which he wanted to run under a narrative that would give the audience the sensation of sitting on a fast train, catching a glimpse of different times and places. He played the section for so many months in the studio that the dancers became weary of it; he made the actual score by layering other sounds over the loop. "Sometimes the sound score is as complex as the dancing."

It took him four months from that bus-top inspiration to the finished piece, working with a group of dancers who were by that time totally in tune with the specialised nature of the movement he required. Shechter likes his dancers to move through the floor as if it is not there, to roll in and out of it as if it were nothing. But he also wants them to feel the weight of their bodies and to progress silently. "Moving quietly helps me to discover the right balance between intensity and looseness in the body." His dancers often travel across the stage with backs curved, hunched forward, heads bowed, arms heavy, fists sometimes clenched. They look both silken and grounded. Watching Shechter at work in the studio David Jays observed how evocative his instructions were. He urged his dancers to look more "gooey", as if they were being smeared into new shapes by a painter's brush. "He speaks often about feeling – not how a move should look, but how it might feel," he reported.[4]

All of this was visible from the moment that *Political Mother* began, with a spotlit image of a despairing soldier committing harakiri to the strains of Verdi's *Requiem*. Cinematically the scene then switched to a massive burst of heavy metal rock guitar and two men raising their arms in supplication; cut again and it was five sinister percussionists hammering their drums; then another tableau which recalled abject prisoners. A demagogue screamed out words of hate; the dancers stamped, leapt and held their heads in unison. "Stunningly," wrote Rupert Christiansen in the *Mail on Sunday*, "Shechter manages to keep up the shock level for the next hour as he puts ten dancers through a dystopian landscape of rage, frustration, anger and violence."[5] Not everyone totally agreed, but all knew that they had witnessed a piece of political, disturbing dance, fuelled by passion and created by a man who was making work like no other.

Here was a choreographer as charismatic as any rock star, taking dance out of its comfort zone and pushing it fiercely onwards. Here was someone who sprang directly from the theatrical tradition of European dance, transmuting it into something different. If people did not readily understand his meaning, if they found his vision too bleak, they could not fail to comprehend the physical impact the pieces made. As David Jays remarked, it is surprisingly rare to see contemporary dance shows that actually make you want to dance. Yet "Hofesh Shechter's work…pulses through the body."[6] By the time he brought the choreographer's cut of *Political Mother* back to Sadler's Wells in 2011, Shechter's company were on a world tour that had taken them to Australasia, the United States, Asia and around Europe. He was a global star.

His abilities mean that he would have achieved this kind of success eventually. But perhaps by then the patina of his originality might have worn thin, or he might have lost confidence in his vision. There is no doubt that Sadler's Wells gave him the opportunity at exactly the right moment. "For the type of work I am doing, the sense of epic size is part of the emotion." He could not have created the same effects in the confines of studio theatres; he is a choreographer who needs the big stage, both literally and metaphorically.

Looking at what was happening at Sadler's Wells in the months around the premiere of *Political Mother* reveals just how many choreographers were by that point beneficiaries of exactly the right kind of exposure. In the week Shechter's piece premiered in Brighton, Sidi Larbi Cherkaoui, another Sadler's Wells associate, was launching his latest work, *Babel*, his third collaboration with Antony Gormley in the theatre's main house. 2010 also saw the return of *Eonnagata*, the revival of Matthew Bourne's *Cinderella*, the debut of Russell Maliphant's full-length *AfterLight*, the London premiere of Akram Khan's *Vertical Road* and the world premiere of Wayne McGregor's *Far*. There were new works from distinguished British choreographers Jonathan Burrows and Rosemary

Above and previous: Hofesh Shechter's *Political Mother*

Butcher. Tanztheater Wuppertal brought *Iphigenie auf Tauris*, Rosas showed off *The Song*. In addition, there were visits from Alvin Ailey, Rambert Dance Company, Birmingham Royal Ballet, Danza Contemporánea de Cuba, Emmanuel Gat and les ballets C de la B.

At the London Coliseum, the Sadler's Wells sponsored Spring Dance was in full bloom, with a memorable revival of Mark Morris Dance Group's masterly *L'allegro, il penseroso ed il moderato*. A new specially commissioned musical revue *Shoes*, written by Richard Thomas and choreographed by Stephen Mear brought a broad splash of satirical comedy and showbiz pizzazz to the theatre; it later moved to the Peacock Theatre for an extended run. Meanwhile Jasmin Vardimon was making a move in

Above: Javier De Frutos and Pet Shop Boys' *The Most Incredible Thing*

the opposite direction with the searing *7734* marking her main house debut.

As the season continued into 2011, the main house at Sadler's Wells boasted new works by William Forsythe and Mats Ek for Sylvie Guillem, a controversial visit from the Canadian Dave St Pierre, and *The Most Incredible Thing*, an ambitious full-length ballet by Javier De Frutos with a score by the Pet Shop Boys – a show which had people queuing round the block. There was also a visit from the BalletBoyz in which they unveiled their exciting young company The Talent.

What is extraordinary about this line-up is the sheer range of new dance it is possible to see at Sadler's Wells. "There's no snobbery involved as there so often is in dance," observed Matthew Bourne. "The theatre just celebrates dance in all in its forms." At the root of that celebration are the artistic associates, who helped Sadler's Wells to transform itself from being a passive receiver of dance to becoming an important and active commissioner of it. Its relationship with each of those associates has developed differently over time. Some, such as the BalletBoyz, lead an independent existence, pursuing their own agenda separate from the theatre, but always returning to show where they have been, and to inject their energy and their vision. Others are tied more strongly into the fabric, their creations providing the artistic focus of each season.

Every new work was not a success; some failed to win critical or audience approval. But an impressive number gathered both, proving that dance could be simultaneously brave – and accessible. The artistic worth of these creations makes the audience trust the theatre and return to see what else might be on offer.

Spalding could not have turned Sadler's Wells into a success story by setting entertaining seat-fillers against auditorium-emptying high art. By commissioning and backing what he liked, and building on success with yet another daring commission, he proved an important point: you do not have to aim for the lowest common denominator to find an audience. If you aspire to create and back the very best, then people will come. "The thing I have discovered is that you must keep your belief," Spalding said.

In sticking to his guns, Spalding has fulfilled many of the aims he outlined in 2005. Sadler's Wells did become an international dance house, "putting something back" into the art form it espoused, sharing its own new creations with the world, and bringing the world to its stage. It did begin to break down barriers: between different forms of dance, between dance and theatre, and between dance and other forms of art. When Janet Street Porter interviewed Spalding in 2004, she bemoaned the fact that dance seemed to have no links with contemporary art at exactly the moment that British artists were regarded as the best in the world. By 2012, artists were queuing up to design for the dance stage and Spalding could claim a link between the two developments. "Historically, English culture has always been about text, about theatre," he told the *Observer*. "We are moving away from that…we are now more visually literate. It is no coincidence that the two art forms which are growing are the most visual – the visual arts and dance."[7]

That spirit of adventure, a desire to push dance ever onwards, continued as the theatre considered its future – and the future of dance in Britain. Its faith in the next generation made it the natural home for the National

Youth Dance Company, a company created in 2012 with money from the Arts Council and the Department of Education to allow talented young dancers to perform innovative work. Associate artist Jasmin Vardimon is its first guest artistic director.

Conscious that young choreographic talent also needed more support than it was getting, in autumn 2012 Spalding unveiled a line-up of "New Wave" associates, choreographers and creators who were just on the cusp of success in an eclectic range of dance forms from contemporary to hip hop and flamenco. In announcing their appointment, Spalding pointed out that it was up to the theatre itself to guide such young talents. "There has been a lot of emphasis recently on training dancers," he said. "But creating artists is a whole other thing."

Those words are an unconscious echo of something de Valois once said. In 1934, she contributed an article to *The Operatic Association Gazette*. "Creative ability is personal to the individual; it can be trained and guided, but it cannot be made. And the creative mind can easily wear itself out if it does not receive guidance and help." She was thinking of the assistance needed by young dancers but her words could just as easily be applied to the choreographers she nurtured and helped to develop. "The real test of ability is endurance and progress," she added.

The Sadler's Wells of today is very different from the theatre she knew. But like her, it puts the support of creativity and the careful cultivation of artistry at the heart of all it does. Since 2005, Sadler's Wells has nourished a generation of choreographers. Here now comes the future.

Right: Javier De Frutos and Pet Shop Boys'
The Most Incredible Thing

All quotations, unless otherwise stated, from interviews with author.

Chapter One

1   *The Times* December 1, 2006
2   Kathrine Sorley Walker, *Ninette de Valois: Idealist without Illusions*
3   As above
4   Dennis Arundell, *The Story of Sadler's Wells*
5   Ninette de Valois, *Come Dance with Me*
6   As above
7   Kathrine Sorley Walker, as above
8   Brochure for reopening
9   As above
10 Fiona Maddocks, *Evening Standard* March 11, 2005
11 Interview with Debra Craine, *The Times* December 11, 2006
12 Figures from Dance UK
13 Arts Council England
14 *Independent* June 8, 2007
15 *The Times* December 21, 2009
16 *The Times* December 11, 2006

Chapter Two

1   Interview with Debra Craine, *The Times* April 2, 2005
2   Bloomberg Encounters April 28, 2005
3   Luke Jennings, *Observer* June 1, 2008
4   Interview with Debra Craine, *The Times* April 2, 2005, as above
5   Interview in *Daily Telegraph* Australia January 8, 2007
6   *The Stage* July 1, 2005
7   Judith Mackrell, *Guardian* July 13, 2005
8   Ditto
9   Interview with Jean H Lee for the Associated Press July 12, 2005

Chapter Three

1   Interview with Lyndsey Winship, *Independent* April 20, 2005
2   Interview with Diane Solway, *New York Times* October 8, 2006
3   Interview with George Acock for book
4   Jenny Gilbert, *Independent on Sunday* October 3, 2004
5   Judith Mackrell, *Guardian* September 30, 2004
6   Debra Craine, *The Times* November 20, 2003
7   Interview with author, *Telegraph* Magazine Features, not used in printed text

8   *Daily Telegraph* October 4, 2005
9   Debra Craine, *The Times* October 3, 2005
10 Interview with author, *Daily Telegraph* September 9, 2006
11 Judith Mackrell, *Guardian* March 4, 2009
12 Interview with author, *Daily Telegraph* February 18, 2009
13 *Daily Telegraph* July 7, 2011

Chapter Four

1   *Daily Telegraph* June 8, 2012
2   Clement Crisp, *Financial Times* June 10, 2012
3   *Guardian* July 4, 2009
4   *Daily Telegraph* February 15, 2008
5   *Sunday Times* July 19, 2009
6   Sanjoy Roy, *Guardian* November 24, 2008
7   Luke Jennings, *Observer* November 28, 2010
8   Ismene Brown, *Daily Telegraph* November 21,1998
9   *Daily Telegraph* October 13, 2006
10 Debra Craine, *The Times* October 22, 2010
11 *Daily Telegraph* November 23, 2011
12 The Arts Desk November 5, 2012
13 Bloomberg Encounters, April 28, 2005

Chapter Five

1   *Daily Telegraph* May 23, 2012
2   Interview with Allen Robertson, *The Times* November 7, 1995
3   Judith Mackrell, *Guardian* November 16, 1995
4   Allen Robertson as above
5   Nigel Reynolds, *Daily Telegraph* May 8, 1999
6   Interview in Alastair Macaulay: *Matthew Bourne and His Adventures in Dance*, revised edition 2011
7   Interview with author for *Telegraph* Magazine, November 26 2012
8   As above
9   *Guardian*, December 8, 2012
10 Quoted by Debra Craine, *The Times* November 15, 2010
11 Interview with Alice Jones, *Independent* November 18, 2005
12 *Daily Telegraph* December 9, 2010

Chapter Six

1   Quoted by Luke Jennings, *Observer* January 2, 2011
2   David Jays, *Sunday Times* November 7, 2010
3   Judith Mackrell, *Guardian* March 4, 2002
4   *Highbury and Islington Express* February 22, 2002
5   Interview with Alice O'Keefe, *New Statesman* April 7, 2008
6   Ditto
7   David Jays, *Sunday Times* April 13, 2008
8   Luke Jennings, *Observer* April 13, 2008

Chapter Seven

1   *Financial Times* May10, 2008
2   Interview with author, *Daily Telegraph* February 3, 2007
3   Interview with Charlotte Cripps, *The Independent Review* April 27, 2004
4   Ditto
5   *Financial Times* May 22, 2004
6   *Observer* October 30, 2011
7   *Guardian* February 6, 2012

Chapter Eight

1   Kathrine Sorley Walker, *Idealist Without Illusions*
2   Filmed interview with the *Guardian* 2009
3   Interview with author, *Daily Telegraph* October 15, 2009
4   Mark Brown, *Guardian* January 5, 2007
5   Debra Craine, *The Times* September 10, 2007
6   Luke Jennings, *Observer* September 30, 2007
7   *Daily Telegraph* September 21, 2007
8   Interview with author, *Daily Telegraph* September 26, 2008
9   Interview with author, *Daily Telegraph* October 15, 2009
10 Ismene Brown, The Arts Desk October 25, 2009
11 *Daily Telegraph* October 27, 2009
12 Judith Mackrell, *Guardian* May 4, 2010

Chapter Nine

1   Serge Lifar, quoting Diaghilev, quoted in Joy Melville, *Diaghilev and Friends*
2   *The Times* October 16, 2009
3   Interview with author, *Daily Telegraph* October 2, 2009.
4   Ditto
5   *Guardian* October 15, 2009
6   *Financial Times* October 16, 2009
7   Interview with Brian Logan, *Independent* March 13, 2011
8   *Guardian* December 18, 2008
9   *Evening Standard* October 16, 2009
10 Interview with author for *Daily Telegraph*, October 2009, quote unused before
11 Interview with author for *Daily Telegraph* November 29, 2011
12 Luke Jennings, *Observer* October 7, 2007

Chapter Ten

1   Gerald Dowler, *Financial Times* October 5, 2007
2   Mark Monahan, *Daily Telegraph* October 2, 2007
3   Debra Craine, *The Times* October 2, 2007
4   David Jays, *Sunday Times* July 10, 2011
5   Rupert Christiansen, *Mail on Sunday* September 26, 2010
6   David Jays, *Sunday Times* July 10, 2011
7   Quoted by Ruaridh Nicoll, *Observer* December 5, 2012

Photographer Index

Bill Cooper 37, 38, 41, 42, 44, 46, 47, 51, 58, 59, 60, 62, 64, 65, 92, 94, 96, 99, 100, 102

Ravi Deepres 68, 70, 73, 75, 76, 77, 111, 112

Hugo Glendinning 108

Richard Haughton 6, 30

Jane Hobson 85

Derek Kendall © English Heritage 14

Tristram Kenton Front & back cover, 23, 24, 26, 29, 32, 34, 48, 50, 53, 56, 84, 87, 104, 106, 109, 116, 118, 120, 123, 124, 126

Belinda Lawley 8, 80, 81, 83, 88

James Morgan 61

Johan Persson 110

Laurent Philippe 2, 90

Sadler's Wells Archive/Finsbury Library Local History Centre 10, 11, 12

Sasha/Stringer/Hulton Archive/Getty Images 16

Rick Senley 19

Morley Von Sternberg 17, 20

With thanks to

Alistair Spalding and everyone at Sadler's Wells whom I interviewed for this book. George Acock provided assiduous research and Abigail Desch unflagging patience.

Kingsley Jayasekera kept the project rolling.

Charles Glanville and James Hogan of Oberon Books gave good advice.

At the *Daily Telegraph*, my editor Tony Gallagher gave me the time to write and my colleagues on the arts desk took the strain in my absence, particularly Andrew Pettie, Paul Gent and Ben Secher.

My fellow dance critic Mark Monahan kindly read an early manuscript.

Susan Oudot and Paul Forty offered wise words.

Jane Shilling provided detailed notes which were as helpful as her constant encouragement.

My husband Icaro was a champion; he and my sons Augusto and Teodoro put up with a wife and mother who kept vanishing to write.

My brother Simon shouldered many of the tasks I ignored in order to complete the text.

Finally my mother, to whom this book is dedicated, and who died just as I was embarking upon it. She saw Ninette de Valois' Vic-Wells ballet, and it made her love dance: she passed that passion on to me. For that, as for so much else, I think of her every day.